# SPECIAL COMMANDO

*By the same author*:

Night Train to Innsbruck
A Talent to Survive

# Special Commando

The Wartime Adventures of
Lt-Col Robert Wilson, DSO and Bar

REX WOODS

WILLIAM KIMBER. LONDON

First published in 1985 by
WILLIAM KIMBER & CO. LIMITED
100 Jermyn Street, London, SW1Y 6EE

ISBN 0-7183-0570-1

Typeset by Grove Graphics
and printed in Great Britain by
The Garden City Press Limited,
Letchworth, Hertfordshire, SG6 1JS

Special Commando *is dedicated to all the brave submarine captains and crews who, at the height of battle for the Mediterranean in 1941 and 1942, took Tug Wilson on patrol aboard their vessels and launched him on a succession of daring missions — not forgetting the many who subsequently lost their lives beneath the sea and are 'still on patrol'.*

# Contents

# List of Illustrations

# Illustrations in the Text

# Acknowledgements

First on the list of people to whom thanks are due is Guy Greville, MC, since it was his telephone call, following the publication of *Night Train to Innsbruck*, that led me to Tug Wilson's story. I am deeply grateful to Guy Greville, not only for putting me on to Tug Wilson, but also for providing me with his own escape story, which had not previously appeared.

Likewise I would like to thank Bill Atkinson, a Gurkha officer in World War 2, for contacting me and supplying me with information and a photograph of a former tea-planting colleague in Ceylon and fellow Gurkha officer, Peter McDowall, which I was delighted to receive and include.

I was delighted, too, when 'Pip' Gardner, VC, MC, suddenly cropped up while I was writing the last two chapters of *Special Commando*, and provided me so willingly with help and utmost co-operation over important details. One of the great pleasures of researching authentic escape stories is that it brings one into contact with charming and distinguished people – as typified by 'Pip' Gardner.

Similarly, The Very Reverend Canon Desmond Haslehust has provided what strikes me as a most exciting chapter on his own original method of leaving a cattle-truck and his fate thereafter, which supplies an interesting variation on the escaping theme. To him, too, I am most grateful.

I would like to acknowledge the help and inspiration that I derived from reading the excellent book by C. B. Courtney, MBE, MC, (Robert Hale) '*S.B.S. in World War II*', which contained a chapter on Tug Wilson. It proved a good basis on which to build. I also want to thank him for the photograph of Tug Wilson leaving Buckingham Palace in July 1942, after receiving his DSO.

To Colonel Sam Derry, DSO, MC, leader of the Rome Organisation for escaped prisoners-of-war, and author of *The Rome Escape Line*, I am also very grateful for many useful and authentic facts provided.

Grateful thanks are also rendered to Henry Brown MBE, General Secretary of the Commando Association, for information supplied and help again kindly provided.

Finally I would like to express my gratitude to Tug Wilson himself, together with his wife, Marjorie, for allowing me to piece together his remarkable story, at a time when he was still convalescing after a major operation and at the same time helping his wife through the after-effects of a subsequent and equally major operation. I sincerely hope that their patience over my questioning, endured at a time of great stress, will be in some measure rewarded by the emergence of *Special Commando*.

Seaton, Devon                                                        Rex Woods
1985

# 'Guy Greville speaking. . . . '

Not long after the publication of my previous book, *Night Train to Innsbruck*, I received two telephone calls, separated by only a few days.

The first was from W. B. Atkinson, a retired Ceylon tea-planter, who had just read a review of *Night Train to Innsbruck*, which mentioned a particularly brave act performed on a train carrying prisoners-of-war in cattle-trucks from Italy to Germany in September 1943, after the Italian armistice with the Allies. The description sounded so exactly like the story of a friend of his in the Gurkhas that he felt sure it must be referring to Peter McDowall, the friend in question. I replied that his friend might well have done something similar and equally brave in another truck or on another train, of which there were several making the journey through the Brenner Pass around that time, but that the name of the officer in *Night Train to Innsbruck* was definitely Guy Greville, as stated in the book. We left it at that, though he was still surprised at the similarity of the two stories.

Then, not many days later, came a second call. When I picked up the receiver and gave my name, a clear voice the other end said: 'This is Guy Greville speaking'. I was delighted because, when I had been preparing the book about a year previously, I had searched in vain for Guy Greville, who plays a most gallant part in the story. With insufficient information available to trace him, I had given up the search and decided to rely on the vivid account of Sherard Veasey, the book's central figure, of the cattle-truck journey that was taking him as a prisoner-of-war through the Brenner Pass to Germany, shortly after the Italian armistice in that fateful September of 1943.

Yet I had expressed two hopes: that what I had written with Sherard Veasey's help was correct (having been on the same train myself, I had no reason to doubt it), and that, with luck, the emergence of the book might bring to light the whereabouts of Guy Greville – preferably alive! Now he had surfaced, loud and clear on the end of

13

the telephone and living not too far away, in Polperro in Cornwall, where he is a staunch District Councillor.

I immediately sent him a copy of *Night Train to Innsbruck*, which was no more than he deserved, in view of the very courageous part that he played in that story. Then to my great relief he rang up to say that he had read the book and that the story was correct, except for one point. In the book I had described how he had performed an act of great courage and agility, thereby releasing several of his fellow-prisoners, and I had said that he had had to perform that feat not once but twice, through force of circumstances which will emerge in the course of this present book. He modestly pointed out that he was so exhausted after his first effort that a friend of his (alas long since deceased) called Peter McDowall, volunteered to perform the feat on the second occasion. Guy Greville was now anxious to set the record straight, in honour of Peter McDowall's memory and for the sake of his family. Here I would like to add that it is perhaps not surprising that it was thought that it was Guy Greville who had performed the feat on both occasions, in view of the fact that it not only occurred more than forty years ago, but also in pitch darkness, and that the two men were of similar size. Nevertheless I welcomed the chance to set the record straight.

I was also glad to be able to ring W. B. Atkinson and tell him that he was indeed right, and I was also able to pass on a little information from Guy Greville concerning Peter's death not long after his successful escape to Switzerland, which is described in this book, in the chapter entitled 'Dolomite Journey'.

To Guy Greville I mentioned that the best chance of setting the record straight might be in a future book, including the hitherto untold story of Guy's own escape after leaving the train (accompanied by Peter McDowall and others). I asked casually if he had any other escapes to his credit and was interested to hear that he had indeed carried out an earlier escape, from Sulmona Camp in Italy, with Captain (later Lieutenant-Colonel) Robert ('Tug') Wilson, DSO and Bar.

Through the Commando Association I obtained Lieutenant-Colonel Wilson's address and found out that he had served in the Special Boat Section of the Commandos from 1940, and that he had been one of the earliest volunteers to answer Winston Churchill's call for shock troops who would 'set Europe ablaze'. Tug Wilson started with the Mediterranean as the scene for his special conflagrations.

Further research revealed that, though Tug Wilson was frequently mentioned in various war books, his own wartime exploits had yet to be fully told as a true story in their own right. All that was needed was his permission and co-operation, both of which were fortunately forthcoming.

Thus it was that Guy Greville's telephone call led not only to the writing of the story of Tug Wilson's deeds of valour in World War II, but also the inclusion of Guy Greville's own successful escape in the company of his friend Peter McDowall from the same train as that from which Tug Wilson also absconded in Modena station.

Almost at the same time that Guy Greville surfaced and Bill Atkinson telephoned about Peter McDowall, I was invited out to lunch to meet The Very Reverend Desmond Haslehust (sic – not Haslehurst) who had just read *Night Train to Innsbruck* and wanted to meet me. It turned out that he, too, when Captain Haslehust of the Worcestershires, had also made a successful exit from the train in question. As his method and consequences differed from those of the others, his adventures too have found a worthy place in *Special Commando*.

One of the fascinations of writing true war stories is that one escape seems to lead to another. Furthermore the research involved in piecing the stories together has led me to explore or re-visit very interesting places, and to meet equally interesting people – and to appreciate how lucky I am to be able to do so. It is a pleasure that I hope I can share with readers of Tug Wilson's story in *Special Commando*.

CHAPTER 1

# Explosion under Etna

The date was 28th June 1941, in the middle of a hot summer; the theatre of war was the Mediterranean, at a point off the east coast of Sicily; the stage back-drop against which a reverberating drama was about to be enacted was mighty Mount Etna, rising stark in the distance and clearly visible through the periscope of one of His Majesty's submarines, on patrol from its base on Malta.

HM S/M *Urge*, under Lieutenant-Commander 'Tommo' Tomkinson, was on patrol in what was known by submariners as a 'billet' off the coast of Sicily, searching for Axis shipping being used to supply Rommel and his Afrika Korps. An additional assignment was to land and retrieve two members of the Special Boat Section of the Commandos, by using a folding canoe, known as a folboat (originally spelled folbot), with a view to carrying the war to Italian soil. This was in pursuance of Winston Churchill's avowed policy of harassing the enemy, both Germans and Italians, with assorted raids at selected points along their coastlines. The idea was to use the submarine for a shoreline reconnaissance, cruising submerged and looking through the periscope for likely targets for destruction near the coast.

The Captain's attention focussed on to a tempting railway-line that appeared to run along the Sicilian coast, between Taormina and Catania, almost at the foot of Mount Etna, before disappearing into a tunnel through a rocky promontory. This seemed a promising target and the Special Boat Section officer on board, a lieutenant in the Royal Artillery, was hastily summoned to the periscope to have a look. He enthusiastically agreed that the prospects looked favourable – at any rate from four miles off the coast, which was as close as it was wise to venture by day. The lieutenant took bearings on his compass, confirmed with the Captain that this was the place to land after dark, and set about preparing himself and his partner, a Marine now serving with the Special Boat Section, for action that night.

When darkness finally descended, they lifted their folding canoe

16

through the fore-hatch, on to the deck of the submarine. They replaced the transverse frame, which had been removed to enable the canoe to be passed through the hatch. They then had to load up their explosives and fuses, which were in water-proof and bullet-proof holders, together with their sub-machine guns, loaded ready for immediate use, if necessary. When they were ready and seated in the canoe, the submarine advanced quietly to within little more than a mile from the shore, before submerging slowly, thus allowing the two canoeists to float off on their own.

This was the moment they had been training and waiting for. They paddled cautiously towards the shore, over a calm Mediterranean sea, with virtually no surf to negotiate. It was essential to ply their paddles gently, in order to avoid stirring up the water and creating a tell-tale amount of phosphorescence, which could alert anyone watching from the shore. But their immediate concern was to work their way round several Italian fishing-boats that they encountered. The landing had been timed to avoid the added chance of detection which the moonlight would bring later on. As it was, in the darkness they managed to work their way cautiously past the Italian fishing-boats and reach the shore without any incident. They landed at a point where the beach consisted mainly of shingle and sand, with some convenient rocks next to which they temporarily dumped their considerable load of explosives, and hid their canoe.

The next task was to clamber stealthily up the beach and thence up a steep embankment, at the top of which the two men found the railway-line that they had sighted in the distance earlier in the day. Sure enough the line disappeared into a tunnel leading through a rocky promontory. Better still, the line was a single track, which meant that from whichever direction the first train came, it was bound to trigger off the required explosion – provided that the charges were properly laid. Although the two men were not Sappers, they were well-trained in explosives.

The tunnel was unguarded, as they had thought, and no time was lost in ferrying the explosives up from the beach. The lieutenant chose a point some thirty yards inside the tunnel to lay the charges undisturbed. The gelignite was buried out of sight in position under the sleepers, and dual-purpose ignition studs were laid flush with the under-side of the rail – ready to set off an almighty explosion as soon as a train passed over it.

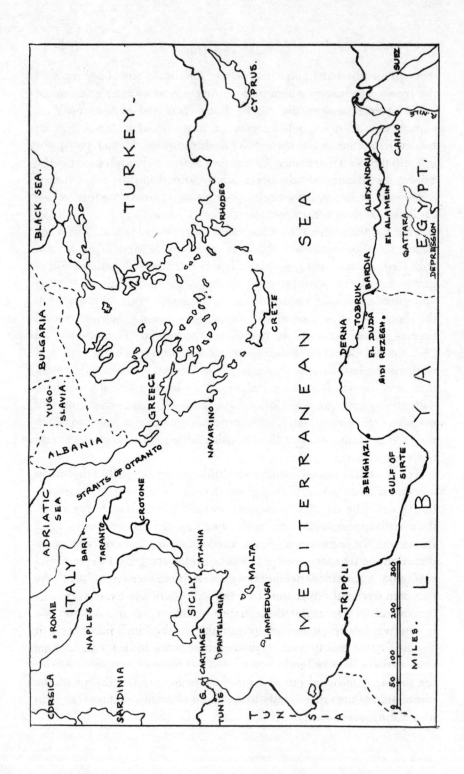

With their job completed in what they hoped was a fool-proof manner, it was time for the two men to remove themselves from the scene of impending uproar and make their way back to the waiting submarine. They moved cautiously down the embankment and the beach, to the canoe hidden behind a rock. They launched it into the sea and followed their compass-bearing to find the submarine, which was waiting anxiously for them.

By now their eyes were working well in the dark and it wasn't necessary for the canoeists to risk shining the torch which was always carried to help them keep their rendezvous. *Urge* was soon sighted to starboard and in a short time the two men had been welcomed back aboard, with the canoe safely stowed away, confident that they had been neither seen nor heard throughout the escapade.

It had been an exhilarating experience and all that was now needed to crown their efforts was the sound of a train approaching, followed, they confidently hoped, by an explosion to signal their success.

They didn't have to wait long, because, as the lieutenant was refreshing himself in the wardroom, he was called urgently up to the bridge on the conning-tower, just in time to see the dim lights of a darkened train approaching the tunnel at the far end, before disappearing into it. A few breath-taking moments later there was a muffled rumble of a big explosion from inside the tunnel.

It was now time for the submarine to submerge and make itself scarce, with the Captain virtually certain that this landing had met with success. But, just to make sure, he kept his craft submerged in the vicinity the next day and kept a constant watch on the tunnel. Two satisfactory observations were made: first, no trains were sighted running in either direction along the railway-line; secondly, breakdown gangs appeared and were seen to be working feverishly at removing the debris from the scene of the explosion. There was now absolutely no room for doubt over the complete success of the wrecking of the coastal railway track for some time to come.

The whole exploit was really an historic occasion, marking as it did the first success in a sabotage operation by personnel of the Special Boat Section in the Mediterranean. There would be more to follow, not only in the Mediterranean but later in the Far East. The Special Boat Section of the Commandos had certainly started with a resounding bang!

However, *Urge*'s patrol was by no means over yet. But before we rejoin her for the remainder of her eventful journey back to base on Malta, it is necessary to go back a little in time, and see how on earth a gunner and a Marine came to be going to war in a submarine – an environment which neither of them, especially the gunner, could have envisaged when they originally volunteered for service with the armed forces. One most certainly wouldn't have expected to encounter a gunner operating in a canoe from a submarine, and carrying out a sapper's job with explosives.

But these were two very remarkable men. Their names were Lieutenant Robert ('Tug') Wilson (RA) and his partner on this and many other missions, Marine W. G. Hughes.

CHAPTER 2

# Christmas Day in a Workhouse

Most ex-servicemen, as well as a good many rugger-club members at after-match parties, have heard of 'Christmas Day in the Workhouse' as recited in a marginally bawdy ballad on the subject. In 1939 Second-Lieutenant Robert Wilson (inevitably known in the Services as 'Tug' – the fate of most Wilsons) actually ate his Christmas pudding in a workhouse – and a condemned one at that!

When the war clouds gathered menacingly and inexorably over Europe, after Neville Chamberlain's visit to Hitler at Berchtesgaden in September 1938, buying time by giving way over Czechoslovakia, Tug Wilson was working as a draughtsman in the Bristol Aeroplane Company. Like many other young men in their twenties, he felt it his duty to volunteer for service in the Territorial Army. Eventually he was commissioned at the age of twenty-seven on 29th August 1939 in the 5th Survey Regiment of the Royal Artillery, on the strength of his proficiency as a draughtsman, with an immediate call-up. He was billeted in a workhouse in Stroud – a condemned and disused building on a windy hill on the outskirts of the town. The place was draughty in the extreme and had a thoroughly Dickensian atmosphere about it.

Here, in Gloucestershire, the 5th Survey Regiment was formed from scratch, with several officers recalled from World War I, and recruits largely from Bristol, including a high proportion of potential officers.

The primary task of the officers was to train this promising material in the theory of survey, the laying out and positioning of guns, and the use of the 3½ inch micrometer theodolite. The work was arduous for the instructors, but on 17th November 1939, Tug Wilson found time for a hurried wedding (with permanent results, it is pleasing to add) to a former Royal Army Service Corps officer's daughter, Marjorie Georgina Thompson by name. Her parents lived in Clifton, Bristol, where she and Tug had known each other for a year. They had a brisk wartime wedding at the Registry Office in Bristol, followed

21

by a short honeymoon in Bath – and then it was back, alone, to
the workhouse for a reluctant Tug. Fortunately Marjorie, having been
born in Aldershot and having spent years in Germany and Egypt with
her parents in the Army, understood the separations entailed in life
in the Services and was prepared to accept them – as indeed she
needed to be for the next eighteen years. Maybe the enforced absences
made the heart grow fonder and the marital bond all the firmer?

Soon after Christmas, Tug Wilson, with his keenness for getting
on with the war by no means diminished by his recent marriage, as
has been known to happen, volunteered for service with the British
Expeditionary Force in France. In March he was posted to the
3rd Survey Regiment of the Royal Artillery, which was again a
predominantly Bristol-raised unit. The Regiment was part of III Corps
– Corps troops, in fact. Its components were dotted around the Corps
area in such familiar World War I places as Amiens, and Armentières,
with a weekly visit to Arras for a much-needed mobile bath. Tug
Wilson's own billet was in Laventie, near Amiens.

Here his time was taken up with fixing gun positions, triangulation
and selecting locations for sound-ranging, whereby the location of
enemy guns could be worked out by the sound waves they made. But
all this smacked more of the kind of static warfare that had been
experienced in World War I than the mobile blitzkrieg which was
soon to be suddenly unleashed by the Germans. For Tug Wilson,
and everybody else in the British Expeditionary Force in France, the
balloon went up on 10th May 1940.

This attack provided Tug Wilson with his first taste of being dive-
bombed and constant retreating – at times on roads or tracks parallel
to the advancing German armour. Finally, he received orders to make
for Dunkirk in his 15 cwt truck, with a view to evacuation before it
was too late. It turned out that his Survey Regiment was one of the
earlier units of the British Expeditionary Force to be safely evacuated
– in keeping with the overall policy of evacuating units of specialist
troops and their equipment first.

On arrival at Dunkirk, where most of the 3rd Survey Regiment
eventually arrived safely, the first sight that greeted Tug Wilson, which
left an indelible impression on him, was a unit of the Royal Indian
Army Service Corps, complete with their mules and an altogether
immaculate turn-out, despite the harassed scamper to Dunkirk. Unlike

many of the later arrivals who had to wade out from the beaches to the waiting fleet of assorted rescue craft, Tug Wilson's unit was able to embark at a jetty – albeit a dive-bombed and damaged structure.

For Tug, Dunkirk had provided a baptism of fire, and he was by no means shattered by the experience. Far from it – he had found it, as far as he personally was concerned, exhilarating and exciting.

On reaching Dover he was able, thanks to an indulgent telephone operator, to have a generously long conversation with his much-relieved wife who was staying with her parents in Clifton. Tug then moved by train to Camberley for re-assembling the regiment. This was followed by a few days leave, a temporary move to Exeter, and thence to Coed-y-Brenin, just North of Dolgelley (as it was then usually spelled), under Western Command.

Life was now back to the old routine, with the 3rd Survey Regiment, practising and instructing survey in its various aspects, including a bearing traverse of the Barmouth estuary. After the excitement of Dunkirk, this was naturally rather dull for anyone as eager for action as Tug Wilson – though considerably less dull or thwarting than spending an indefinite period of years as a prisoner-of-war in Germany or Poland, which was the fate of a large and less fortunate proportion of the stranded British Expeditionary Force. Tug realised his good fortune, all right, but, like a lot of returned soldiers at that time, he was anxious for an opportunity to strike back at the enemy.

It was, therefore, not surprising that, when a call came from Western Command Headquarters for volunteers for 'special service of a hazardous nature', Tug Wilson handed in his name as a volunteer without hesitation.

This call came at the instigation of Winston Churchill, who was anxious to build up a cadre of shock troops for use in striking at the enemy, probably by seaborne landings, in an effort to carry out at least some sort of offensive action against an enemy who now had spread his tentacles over nearly the whole of conquered Western Europe. The Germans and the Italians now had a long coastline to guard and it was Churchill's intention to force them to employ a lot of their troops to protect it from attack. At the same time, while the British army was in the process of re-equipping itself, as well as attending, urgently but only to the limit of its insufficient weapons, to the very real threat of invasion, with no immediate prospect of any large-scale re-occupation of territory in Europe, it was important to mount at least some aggressive action upon the shores of enemy-occupied Europe. In this manner, not only would essential experience for subsequent larger landings be gained, but also the hard-pressed and success-starved civilian population would at least have something in the way of offensive land-action to cheer, as they worked to produce more arms and equipment.

To this end, Churchill issued his famous call for volunteers to 'set Europe ablaze', in the summer of 1940.

Churchill's sentiments met with the full approval of Tug Wilson, and he answered the call as soon as he received it. As is often the case, nothing was heard immediately, but early in November 1940, Tug found himself on the way to the Isle of Arran, off the west coast of Scotland, to join Number 8 Commando – of which he knew practically nothing. At this early stage even the name 'Commando' wasn't yet in general use.

He arrived in the officers' mess at the Duke of Montrose's shooting lodge, called The White House, at Lamlash, on the Isle of Arran. While he was waiting and wondering what the future held for him, and where he would be sent the next day, he sat as a newly-arrived subaltern listening with mounting interest to an older and more mature officer (but still a subaltern at that stage) from the King's Royal Rifle Corps, expatiating to a group of listeners about the enormous potential of the canoe as a means of carrying out successful raids on enemy coasts.

Tug Wilson became more and more captivated by the theories advanced by this imposing officer, who had evidently had extensive canoeing experience, on the Danube and the Nile shortly before the war. In fact he had actually spent his honeymoon paddling down the Danube with his new and venturesome bride. He had also been a big-game hunter in East Africa, before going down the Nile by canoe from Lake Victoria to the Delta. The necessity to earn a living had led him to join the Palestine Police, where he reached the rank of sergeant. He was clearly a man of experience, compared with the average subaltern in 1940, as well as possessing an imposing appearance and physique. He was, at the age of nearly forty, a compelling talker among his younger audience.

When the conversation, which had become virtually a monologue, was ended, Tug Wilson buttonholed this charismatic officer, eager to hear more. The officer in question was Roger Courtney, who had just been appointed to form the Folboat Section of 8 Commando (later to be established on its own and known as the Special Boat Section). His appointment raised him to the rank of captain. During the conversation, which lasted well into the night, a mutual liking and respect was soon established between the two men. The upshot of this was that Roger Courtney offered to take on Tug Wilson as his second-in-command. He had already selected ten other ranks from volunteers for the Commandos, from a wide range of units, including the Grenadier Guards, Royal Marines, Royal Artillery and the Royal Army Service Corps. In addition he had acquired a 'fleet' of eight folboats, one of which was the famous *Buttercup* in which he had completed the Danube journey.

Thus overnight Tug Wilson had switched from his surveyor's theodolite to a canoe and, quite by chance (though entirely voluntarily and with great enthusiasm) he had become a foundation member of a unit that was destined to wreak havoc upon the enemy (as yet unspecified) out of all proportion to its size.

Now it was time to get down to learning the skills of manoeuvering a canoe, including above all getting nimbly in and out without capsizing it. They also had to become proficient in a short space of time with the explosives that they would be using shortly. There was already talk of a quick call to action – in fact a goodly selection of rumours to choose from!

# CHAPTER 3

# 'Layforce'

Lieutenant-Colonel John Durnford-Slater, DSO, was at pains to stress that, when selecting officers and men for his 3 Commando, which fought with distinction at Lofoten, Dieppe, North Africa and Sicily, before eventually playing a prominent part in the D-Day and subsequent fighting in Normandy and into Germany itself, he disregarded mere size as a requirement. He looked for determination, courage and keenness for action in his officers and men. Size might be useful in pub brawls but not in battle, unless it is accompanied by the necessary fighting spirit. Durnford-Slater himself, though a dashing and courageous horseman over fences in between the wars, was no Errol Flynn in size and looks. He fully realised that good Commandos, officers and men alike, came in various sizes and shapes – provided that they had the right basic attributes.

Similarly, Captain Roger Courtney, though himself a man of considerable physical presence, didn't look for the swaggering or outwardly tough type of Commando. He preferred the alert and sensitive type, who would be able to work his way round danger when approaching an enemy coast – rather than attempt to blast his way through. Equally he had no use for the hesitant type, either. For him, as for Durnford-Slater, size was immaterial. What he looked for was determination and enthusiasm for the job in hand, coupled with the skill, coolness and unflappability required to bring success to the kind of clandestine operation that he had in mind for his new Folboat Section.

Tug Wilson, at 5ft 7½ ins in height and less than 10 stones in weight, was by no means in appearance the popularly accepted image of a Commando. Nevertheless he suited Roger Courtney perfectly as his second-in-command. They complemented each other admirably, as time was soon to prove. Courtney could rely on Tug to supervise the training while he himself was away selling the idea of the Folboat Section in the right quarters, with his persuasive tongue, backed up by some convincing personal demonstrations of how to sneak through guarded areas and affix crosses on ships' hulls, to denote the sticking of imaginary limpets.

Now the immediate task was to start training in order to acquire the necessary expertise in the use of their canoes, particularly by night. For this purpose they were billeted in Corrie, on the east coast of the Isle of Arran, near the northern end of the island. Goat Fell rose steeply behind them to a height of 2,817 feet, with Sannox Bay in front of them, providing an ideal, if sometimes rather frightening, training area for canoeists. All training was carried out in battle-dress. Wet-suits were not yet in vogue and weren't issued; nor were life-belts! At night it was very dark – just as it would be on real operations, since they would have to operate with as little moonlight as possible, so as to remain as invisible as they could. The newly formed Folboat Section had to develop its canoeing skills quickly.

It was here that the Folboat Section received a visit from Admiral Sir Roger Keyes, of Zeebrugge fame, in his capacity of Chief of the Commandos. Sir Roger seemed impressed with what he found, as well as by the considerable potential, and especially the comparative effectiveness of raids by canoe, to be carried out by a mere handful of trained men wreaking a disproportionate amount of havoc on enemy coasts.

Here, too, the members of the Folboat Section received their first instructions in the handling of explosives – a vital necessity if their sabotage raids were to reap the hoped-for rewards.

After ten days' leave at Christmas (1940) the Commandos returned to training, amid an increasing buzz of rumours of impending action – which was precisely what they had volunteered for. On 13th January 1941 they were sent on a fortnight's overseas embarkation leave. On 31st January Tug Wilson with the Folboat Section, attached to 8 Commando, boarded the 10,000 ton Commando ship, the HMS *Glenroy*, at Gourock, with the folboats safely stowed aboard. They were part of 'Layforce', consisting of 7, 8 and 11 Commandos, under the command of Lieutenant-Colonel R. E. Laycock. Two other similar Commando ships, HMS *Glengyle* and HMS *Glenearn*, completed the transport.

The strongest rumour as to their destination was that they were going to the Middle East, in preparation for a landing on the island of Rhodes, to follow Wavell's recent successful thrust against the Italian army in Cyrenaica, as far as El Agheila – not that the convoy steered in that direction when it sailed down the Clyde from Gourock. They seemed to be heading out towards the north-west, right out into the North Atlantic, till they were out of range for long-distance bombers. Finally they veered to the south, under heavy escort, and hit the full force of the Atlantic swell. Roger Courtney and Tug Wilson, who were sharing a cabin, had the officers' mess to themselves for breakfast – thanks perhaps to the 'sea legs' that they had already acquired while afloat in their folboats? It seemed a good omen for the future, which held out the prospect of an amphibious life for both of them.

When the swell subsided, the troops settled down to getting to know their weapons, including some newly-issued sub-machine-guns. Poker and bridge also helped to pass the time, until, after a couple of weeks they put into Freetown in Sierra Leone, on the west coast of Africa. Here a notable addition to the party was Captain Randolph Churchill. Layforce already included another son of a famous father, Lieutenant-Colonel Geoffrey Keyes, whose father Admiral Sir Roger Keyes had instigated the whole operation. Geoffrey, alas, was destined to die bravely, when taking part in a Commando raid on Rommel's headquarters at Beda Littoria, in Cyrenaica. Ironically, Rommel wasn't there at the time – he was on leave in Italy.

Nearly a fortnight later the convoy reached a temporary Shangri-La in Cape Town, where they received the cordial welcome extended to Allied convoys throughout the war from the residents of that delightful city beneath Table Mountain. In those days, with South Africa a staunch member of the Commonwealth, under the guidance of General Smuts, the English-speaking community, as well as a good proportion of the Afrikaner population, had thrown in their lot wholeheartedly with Britain and the rest of the Commonwealth in the struggle (alone at that time) against the so-far triumphant Axis powers, and had volunteered for service in large numbers. Some were already fighting in East Africa against Mussolini's troops and were soon to fight in the Western Desert, and later in Italy. Britain was glad of their support then, as was Tug of the rapturous reception accorded to his convoy. When convoys of troopships arrived round the Cape, bound for the Middle East or India, some of the ships called at Cape Town while others went round the coast to Durban. In each case the welcome was the same, with fleets of private cars (on rationed petrol) to meet them and drive them to see the local sights, or sample for a while the comforts of a private home – thus providing a morale-boosting interlude in the long voyage to war for the troops in transit. Many of the survivors returned after the war to settle in that hospitable land.

It was still mid-summer when HMS *Glenroy*, with Tug Wilson aboard, sailed away from their temporary haven in Cape Town. Fortunately, by the time the ships worked their way up the east coast of Africa, via the Mozambique Channel, on past Dar-es-Salaam and Mombasa, and into the Red Sea via Aden, they were moving back into the cool (or, rather, less hot) season. Finally they arrived at Suez, on 7th March 1941. The general relief at safely reaching their destination was expressed in the form of three cheers for the Captain of HMS *Glenroy* from 8 and 11 Commandos combined, for safely steering them over some 14,000 miles of ocean. For its part, the Folboat Section lost no time in getting its canoes out of the hold and going for a training spin round the Gulf of Suez. It was good to get the feel of a paddle again.

But during their weeks at sea, much had happened on the Middle East battlefronts, which was to affect the immediate future of Layforce. First, Rommel and his formidable Afrika Korps had arrived in Tripolitania and had succeeded in driving Wavell's recently victorious, but now overstretched and undersupplied, land forces back beyond the encircled (but not on this occasion captured) port of Tobruk. Secondly, the Italians had been making heavy work of subduing the determined Greeks and Hitler had found it necessary, with his impending attack on Russia in mind, to intervene with his troops and clear up the mess there, too, before striking to the east. The short campaign in Greece was about to start and, far from Wavell being able to contemplate a landing on Rhodes with his newly-arrived Commandos, for which purpose Layforce had been summoned and sent, he was now obliged to send reinforcements, so badly needed in the Desert, to fight in Greece instead. Crete, too, was about to be invaded, and part of Layforce was used in an unavailing attempt to stem the tide there.

The Folboat Section was moved to Geneifa where, to Tug's consternation, all his teeth became loose. He was suffering from an attack of gingivitis, an ailment of the gums, he was told. But he was quickly cured and sent on a week's leave in Cairo, which he spent at the Mena House Hotel, where his parents-in-law were well-remembered from their pre-war service days in Egypt. One of his wife's more unusual trophies is an engraved cup for winning a camel race! On the strength of this remembrance a two-seater Chevrolet and a horse to ride were put at his disposal by the local Chief of Police.

Thus restored, he returned to Geneifa on March 31st, in time to move on with the Folboat Section to an excellent training area at Kabrit, on the shores of the Great Bitter Lake. As second-in-command, Tug organised the training while Roger Courtney was busy knocking on doors – and forcing entry into some important rooms – in General Headquarters in Cairo. He was attempting to gain suitable, and guard against unsuitable, employment for his folboats. His persuasive powers and infectious enthusiasm met with success in certain high places. Roger Courtney was determined that his Folboat Section should be used on raids from submarines on the North African and Italian coasts, for which purpose he had always intended them.

The first fruits of his labours accrued when the Folboat Section was given its official establishment. This was to be: two officers, two sergeants, four corporals, two lance-corporals and eight other ranks, as well as a complement of twelve canoes. This was a step in the right direction – even if, at present, they could only muster one officer nine other ranks and seven canoes. The one officer was Tug Wilson, because Roger Courtney was away on various missions, including an important reconnaissance by submarine and canoe off the coast of Rhodes with Lieutenant-Commander Nigel Clogstoun-Wilmott, RN, of Combined Operations (Middle-East). This strengthened his hand in his public-relations ploys with the Royal Navy, under whom he wanted his Folboat Section to operate.

Then, on 13th April 1941, a milestone was reached in the history of the original Folboat Section – it was taken, with its canoes, aboard the depot ship of the 1st Submarine Flotilla of the Mediterranean Fleet, HMS *Medway*, in the port of Alexandria. Tug Wilson made sure that its full supply of limpets and explosives and detonators went with it. He had personally managed to gather them off HMS *Glenroy* and HMS *Glenearn*. They were thus fully armed and ready for action.

This move gave the Folboat Section what it wanted: an identity of its own; a certain amount of autonomy; and the prospect of action from submarines. It also brought a change of name. From now on the former Folboat Section of the Commandos was to be known as the Special Boat Section, at the disposal of the Royal Navy – and, more immediately, under Captain (Submarines) Raw, RN. Action was not to be long in coming.

CHAPTER 4

# The Brass Lizard

The initial reaction of some naval authorities to having 'Pongos' in their midst was mixed. While they admired the courage of these men in army uniform, with their flimsy folding canoes and their piles of explosives, there was also a feeling around that 'passengers' on board a submarine spelled disaster. Fortunately Roger Courtney had already got on well with the Navy, and vice versa. In particular he had established a good rapport with Admiral Maund, director of Combined Operations at General Headquarters, Middle-East. This helped overcome the antipathy felt by some naval officers who reckoned that the purpose of submarines was to sink ships, and not to be diverted on to special landing operations.

So it was that on 24th April 1941 Tug was summoned before Captain (S) Raw, RN, of Number 1 Submarine Flotilla in Alexandria. He was detailed for patrol in a 'T' class submarine, *Triumph*, under Lieutenant-Commander 'Sammy' Woods (later Admiral Sir Wilfred Woods).

Captain Raw didn't brief Tug as to the site of his forthcoming landing or possible target. Such was the tightness of security on the matter that the choice of target and the precise area was left, on this and all but one of Tug's subsequent landings, to the captain of the submarine that was carrying him. Base, of course, knew what billet a submarine was patrolling and was able to keep in touch. But no pre-arranged landing-spots were established or disclosed.

To add to Tug's equipment, four water-proof watches were sent for by Captain Raw. When, in the course of conversation, Tug mentioned that his wife, Marjorie, was in Bristol, which, according to the latest news from home, had been badly blitzed, Captain Raw said that he would see if he could get any information on the subject, and wished Tug good luck. Tug banished the thought from his mind and concentrated on the task in hand.

This was to be Tug's first trip in a submarine. He chose to take

32

with him as his partner Marine W. G. Hughes, a dark-complexioned Englishman; like Tug Wilson himself, Hughes was of lean and wiry build. He was as keen as mustard to be on the first operation of the new Special Boat Section – as of course was Tug himself. Not for him an organising job as 2 i/c in the background. He was determined to form the spearhead of attack.

Tug took to life on board a submarine like a duck to water. For a start, he was a very convenient size for packing into a submarine, and for keeping out of the way of the rest of the crew as they went about their duties. He soon discovered that submariners were a race apart, and that the discipline was less formal than in any other ship – though effective, none-the-less. Submarine discipline was of necessity based on implicit faith in the captain and his judgement in a crisis, and on instant response to his orders – with each member of the crew knowing his allotted job backwards.

Tug Wilson and Marine Hughes were soon absorbed into the almost family atmosphere of life aboard *Triumph*, and were given certain tasks. Tug helped the engineering officer (referred to as 'the plumber'), who had no watch-keeping duties, with the decoding of messages. He also spent a lot of time preparing and checking his limpets and detonators. Special gloves were needed for handling the blasting gelatine, and a headache was liable to result from prolonged work with this substance. There was also a tendency for the pressure which built up inside a submarine while she was submerged to trouble the ears of some people. For anyone with this kind of ear trouble, or with claustrophobia for that matter, inside a submarine was no place to be. Fortunately for Tug and Marine Hughes, they both took to submarine life and routine with little difficulty.

When off duty, they could play cards or sleep, until 'action stations'. Pontoon was a favourite, as was 'uckers', otherwise known as ludo. Smoking was allowed only when the submarine was on the surface and welcome fresh air was pouring down from the conning-tower – to the relief of all aboard.

Tug gathered at an early stage that, since the early days of submarine warfare in World War I, there had been a complete change of thought in one respect. In World War I it had been regarded as quite an adventure for a submarine to dive. The diving techniques were still being developed. By World War II the opposite applied –

the safest place, particularly in a closed sea like the Mediterranean, for a submarine was underwater, with a return to the surface now regarded as something of an adventure. The use of reconnaissance aircraft had brought about this change of attitude. Consequently submarines, which had to surface in order to re-charge their batteries, did so at night, when there were no reconnaissance planes about. By day, the use of periscopes enabled submarines to reconnoitre without surfacing and being spotted. Each submarine had two periscopes – the main one and a much smaller one for use in attack.

The first minor excitement on Tug's maiden patrol was the sighting of a floating mine, which had to be destroyed by firing on it.

Then, on 3rd May 1941, came Tug's first major excitement. *Triumph* was patrolling the Gulf of Sirte, off the Libyan coast, looking for possible targets among supply ships to Rommel's troops in North Africa. What turned out to be a two-masted Italian copper-bottomed schooner, called the *Tugnin F*, was sighted. A 4-inch shell across her bows made her heave to, and her crew were ordered to get into their life-boat and row over to the submarine. A bunch of exceedingly scared Italians complied with these instructions and were taken on board *Triumph* – looking as if they were sure that their last moment had come. *Triumph*'s captain, Lieutenant-Commander Sammy Woods, ordered the navigating officer and Tug Wilson to use the empty lifeboat and row over to the schooner and board her, in order to examine her cargo, which proved to be mainly macaroni.

Thus Tug, who had started out with the intention of landing and blowing up a worthwhile target, now found himself the first man aboard a captured enemy vessel. He kept a sharp look-out for booby-traps, but luckily found none. He found pictures of Mussolini and Hitler in the captain's cabin, and took down the Italian ensign. These he took, together with the captain's papers from his desk; with them he removed a magnificent brass lizard, over a foot long, which was used as a paper-weight – and now reposes on Tug Wilson's own desk in his home in Leamington Spa!

The two-man boarding-party returned to the submarine, which, as a precaution against possible air attack, had dived to a safe depth while the search of the *Tugnin F* was in progress. As they neared the submarine Tug held up the picture of Hitler for the captain to see through his periscope, as an inducement to surface and take his two 'pirates' back aboard.

The now less frightened Italian crew members were restored to their lifeboat, to make their own way back to shore, while the submarine proceeded to sink the *Tugnin F* by gunfire. This had only just been accomplished when aircraft appeared overhead and *Triumph* had to make a hasty crash-dive.

The rest of the patrol was spent in vain pursuit of ships leaving the North African coast at a speed too fast to allow *Triumph* to catch them. Tug, though happy and exhilarated by his surprise boarding-party role, was still anxious to achieve what he had set out to do – namely, to blow something up on enemy territory.

He was keen to be allowed to try his luck with some limpets in Benghazi harbour, but the captain wisely vetoed his suggestion. The weather was far too rough and the captain insisted that it would be foolhardy to try in such conditions. Tug was naturally disappointed, but was learning that in submarine warfare there are occasions when one has to wait for another day.

On the way back to base at Alexandria, Tug was helping with the deciphering when he came upon the following message: 'To HM Sub *Triumph* from Capt (S) 1 – Please inform Lt Wilson that police Bristol telegraph wife safe and well'. The news itself, plus the fact that Captain (S) Raw had gone to the trouble of obtaining it for his newly attached 'Pongo', made Tug feel more than ever that he was in good hands.

Thus he returned to base in Alexandria in good spirits from his first patrol. It had been by no means uneventful, even if he had come back with his explosives still unused. He had picked up a lot of useful experience, and had a handsome trophy in his pocket – the Brass Lizard!

# CHAPTER 5

# Malta Flotilla

It was decided back at the base of Number 1 Submarine Flotilla that the area where Tug Wilson and his partner Marine Hughes could be most profitably employed was out of Malta. This was where some of the most juicy targets lay, because at this time, the summer of 1941, Rommel's supplies had already taken a bashing from the 10th Submarine Flotilla, operating from the beleaguered island, but were still being sent across to North Africa in large quantities.

Not surprisingly, Malta too was taking an almost daily pasting from Axis bombers, anxious to neutralise and eventually capture this strategic island which was proving such a thorn in Rommel's flesh, in his drive to build up reserves of men and equipment strong enough to carry him through to Alexandria and Cairo, en route for the Suez Canal. But such had been the losses in German and Italian transport ships in the Mediterranean that most of Rommel's supplies now went perforce by the shortest possible route – from Sicily or Southern Italy across to Tripoli. Here they had to contend with the submarines of Number 10 Flotilla, patrolling out of Malta. In 1941 the struggle was very much in the balance.

With the Sicilian coast just visible from Malta on a clear day, this area offered a rich harvest of targets for demolition by Tug Wilson and his partner. But first they had to get there.

The transport chosen for them was a huge mine-laying submarine, aptly named HM S/M *Cachalot* – the name of a large species of whale. If *Triumph* had seemed like a shark, as submarines are often described, then *Cachalot* now seemed by comparison a veritable whale. There was even a bathroom for the captain, Lieutenant-Commander Hugo Newton. So Tug Wilson and Marine Hughes made their way in comparative comfort and space to Malta.

*Cachalot* took with her on board a considerable quantity of stores urgently needed on Malta, including some 18" torpedoes as replacements. Also aboard was a consignment of special medical

supplies for the RAF. One wag in the crew suggested the these were mainly a fresh supply of Brylcream, which was always associated with the well-groomed appearance of the pilots of the RAF! Attempts to keep Malta supplied with fuel and other necessities by surface craft were proving costly. Like Rommel's supply ships to North Africa, the vessels supplying Malta were suffering heavy losses.

On arrival at Number 10 Submarine Flotilla's base, HMS *Talbot* at Lazaretto, on Malta, Tug joined a ward-room where morale was high and the welcome warm. The excellent atmosphere of this mess was largely due, Tug thought, to the captain of the flotilla, Captain (S) G. W. G. Simpson, RN (later Rear Admiral, CB, CBE) whom all the submariners appeared to worship. One of his most endearing gestures was that, no matter at what time a submarine returned from patrol, Captain Simpson ('Shrimp' as he was known) was bound to be at the quayside, together with Commander Sam Macgregor, the chief engineer of the flotilla, to welcome the returning crew.

The submarine base on Malta, the Lazaretto on Manoel Island, was in many ways an excellent headquarters for No 10 Submarine Flotilla – not that it had been originally designed for such a purpose. The building dated back several centuries to the time when it was a quarantine quarters in the days of the bubonic plague. A wing for an isolation hospital had been added later, but the whole place had stood empty for many years. It had much to commend it as a submarine base during World War II, when Malta became a key point in the battle for the Mediterranean.

For a start the Lazaretto was so sited that only a direct hit could damage it seriously. Facing south, it abutted on to the harbour, which contained water to a depth of forty feet and submarines could lie alongside when not out on patrol. The building itself was strongly constructed, being made of limestone blocks and slabs hewn out of the rock behind to the north. This rock gave good protection on the northern side. With deep water in front and high solid rocks behind, the Lazaretto was proof against bombs, barring a direct hit.

The main long building was two storeys high and was sub-divided into four sections by three courtyards with rooms running north and south, thus providing good barracks. At the eastern end, which opened on to the harbour, the former rooms of the isolation hospital were suitable for officers' cabins round a central Mess. A long corridor

ran the whole length of the building on ground- and first-floor levels.
The main entrance was at the west end of the corridor at ground level.
There was also a back door at roof level in the centre of the building
on the northern side, leading to a stone staircase into the rock, where
by means of excavation a bomb-proof shelter had been provided.
Lazaretto was a solid wartime submarine base – as indeed it needed
to be as the enemy bombing intensified in an all-out attempt to put
it out of action.

A time-worn copy of *The Times of Malta*, dated 27th September 1941,
contains the text of a local broadcast made by Captain G. W. G.
Simpson, RN, of the 10th Submarine Flotilla. In stressing the vital
importance of the efficiency of a submarine's captain, he produced
the following rather surprising statistics: In World War I, Germany
lost about 160 submarines and surrendered 170. From these 330
submarines, a mere four German submarine commanders were
responsible for half the Allied shipping sunk. Ten submarine
commanders accounted for seventy-five per cent of Allied losses. In
view of these figures, he pointed out that the sinking or capture
of, say, three of these 'ace' commanders, meant an enormously
disproportionate gain to the other side. He pointed out further that
in the British Navy the level of performance of submarine commanders
was far more even.

He concluded:

Each man in a submarine must not only know how to do his job,
but also understand the diving mechanism of the submarine, and
the position of every important valve, since one mistake on the part
of any member of the crew may cause the vessel's loss. But statistics
show that in no other profession is the success or failure of a powerful
unit so dependent on the judgement or skill of one man – the
captain.

'Shrimp' Simpson certainly had around him, with 10 Flotilla, Malta,
an outstanding team of submarine captains, many of whom, after
winning many decorations for sustained bravery, alas eventually failed
to return – but not before selling their lives dearly in the battle of
the Mediterranean. Tug was to sail in no less than nine submarines
during the eighteen months of his secondment to the Royal Navy as
a member of the Special Boat Section. Both on shore and in action

on patrol Tug Wilson got to know, like and admire these intrepid
men. Largely because of 'Shrimp' Simpson, despite the inevitable
losses that occurred, an atmosphere of impending doom was never
allowed to pervade the ward-room.

When Tug reported for duty, he found that 'Shrimp', too, like some
other senior naval officers, was at first a little sceptical about the
employment of Tug and his explosives as an extra weapon, but decided
to send him on patrol with *Urge*, a U-class submarine, under
Lieutenant-Commander 'Tommo' Tomkinson, to see what he could
do. It was perhaps worth trying! *Urge*, with Tug Wilson, Marine
Hughes and their folboat aboard, set off for the east coast of Sicily.

So it was that a lieutenant in the Royal Artillery and a Royal Marine
found themselves peering through a submarine's periscope, at a
railway tunnel under Mount Etna and listening to the rumble – not
of Mount Etna erupting, but of the mighty explosion that they
themselves had just brought about. This was only the beginning!

*

Not long after *Urge* had moved away from the scene of Tug's (and
indeed the Special Boat Section's) first explosion on enemy soil, the
officer of the watch reported to the captain that there was smoke on
the horizon. The klaxon sounded and there was an immediate call
to 'action stations', and soon the hull of a ship appeared in the
periscope. Submarines carried up-to-date versions of *Jane's Fighting
Ships* and *Jane's Merchant Ships* and in no time the ship on the horizon
was identified, complete with full details of her guns and her crew
members, as a ten-thousand-ton eight-inch Italian cruiser of the
*Gorizia* class. It soon became clear that she was in company with
another ten-thousand-ton eight-inch cruiser, escorted by six destroyers.

This was obviously a most important target, possibly setting out
to attack a vital Allied relief convoy, heading for Malta. No time was
lost in firing four 21-inch torpedoes at one of the two cruisers, which
sank within minutes.

The submarine's captain, Lieutenant-Commander 'Tommo'
Tomkinson, didn't expect to get away with this spectacular success,
without experiencing immediate and prolonged retribution at the

hands of the escort. He issued the order: 'Stand by for depth-charging'. All watertight doors were shut and evasive action below the surface was taken. Tug Wilson remembered Roger Courtney's advice for Special Boat Section personnel during a depth-charge attack. They included advice to be seated, well out of the way, in the control-room or elsewhere, and become, or at least appear, engrossed in a book. Tug found the noise disconcerting and the sensation like a series of blows with a sledge-hammer on the none-too-solid hull of the submarine. After counting ninety bangs he was relieved when it was all over and they were able to finish their patrol before making their way back safely to base on Malta.

It was customary for a submarine returning from a successful 'kill' to hoist a flag with the 'Jolly Roger' skull and crossbones to indicate the success scored. For the sinking of the enemy cruiser there was a bar on the flag, and to this had been added a dagger, specially embroidered to record the first stab at the enemy by members of the Special Boat Section, by means of a successful landing-raid.

Not surprisingly, after this convincing performance, Captain (S) 10 sent a signal to Alexandria, requesting permission for Lieutenant Wilson and Marine Hughes to remain under his command for further duties. His initial doubts had clearly now been resolved! He was anxious for further two-pronged assaults on the enemy.

So, too, was Tug Wilson. Captain Roger Courtney's reply was brief: 'Carte blanche – good hunting'.

# CHAPTER 6

# Setting the Mediterranean Ablaze

Tug Wilson's first big bang, under Mount Etna, coupled with *Urge*'s sinking of the Italian cruiser, sent morale sky high at the submarine base at Lazaretto. Other submarines of the flotilla were having their successes, too, and were all anxious to add to the growing total of enemy shipping sunk by the flotilla. There was no hanging back or resting on laurels for the members of Number 10 Submarine Flotilla on Malta. Relentless pursuit of the enemy remained uppermost in their minds.

As far as Tug was concerned, a swift change in the attitude of Captain (S) 'Shrimp' Simpson had resulted from the first explosion near Etna. The superstition among submarine crews that 'passengers' aboard were an unlucky omen had likewise evaporated with the smoke of the recent explosion, and now Tug Wilson and his partner Marine Hughes were welcome in the submarines of Number 10 Flotilla. By taking Tug Wilson and his explosives aboard they were adding another dimension to the role of a submarine, lending extra purpose and excitement to the long and arduous duty of patrolling.

When Tug Wilson first answered Winston Churchill's historic call 'to set Europe ablaze', he little knew what lay in store for him. All he knew was that he, like other Commandos, wanted to volunteer for action. Now, to his surprise, he was in a position to set the Mediterranean ablaze, just as Churchill wanted. This was a situation that Tug was keen to exploit to the full. Marine Hughes was equally determined to help him do it. There wasn't long to wait.

But first they had to put up with one short-lived frustration. They accompanied *Urge* on her next patrol. It started merrily enough, with the captain, Tommo Tomkinson, opening his mail in the ward-room and announcing that his wife had apparently been telling people in Portsmouth that her husband had now 'got the *Urge*', which amused them all. But before *Urge* had reached her patrol billet, the Captain had got something much more painful – he had got lumbago. This was severe and far from conducive to bending to manipulate the periscope or, for that matter, making the instant decisions that are required of a submarine commander in action. There was nothing for it but to return to base for treatment, and hope for better luck next time.

This proved only a temporary setback, for Tug Wilson and Marine Hughes were soon detailed to accompany HM S/M *Utmost* on patrol. Her captain was Lieutenant-Commander Dick Cayley, a stockily-built and determined officer for whom Tug already had a liking and was soon to develop a great respect. Their patrol billet included the Gulf of Santa Eufemia, off the 'instep' of the 'boot' of Italy.

Tug and Hughes were floated gently off *Utmost* in their canoes, having previously selected their target by day, as usual. They had chosen a stretch of railway-line, which they proceeded to mine with explosives. They hadn't managed to find a tunnel this time, their intention being to cause an explosion on what appeared to be a strategic coastal line of communication. They were able to fix their explosives into position and withdrew to the shelter of some rocks to await the bang.

Suddenly all hell was let loose. There was a mighty explosion, followed by feverish activity along the line as some guardhouses disgorged several exceedingly excited Italian soldiers. As Tug and his partner lay safely concealed and observing, a strange diversion came to their aid most opportunely. It was mid-summer and some nude bathers, of both sexes, were rounded up by the indignant guards, who took them for frog-men saboteurs who had just caused the explosion. While the shouting and the protests continued, Tug and Hughes managed to slip away and launch their canoe unobserved.

Thus Tug Wilson and Marine Hughes brought off their second big bang and justified the addition of another dagger to a ship's 'Jolly Roger' flag.

This success in *Utmost* was followed up by an even bigger and more spectacular demolition, on a large railway bridge over the River Seracino, in the Gulf of Taranto, on the night of 27/28th August 1941. Again they were on patrol with *Utmost*, under Lieutenant-Commander Dick Cayley.

This time they were out for a really large and vital target, for which a maximum amount of explosive was obviously going to be needed.

A thorough periscope reconnaissance was made by daylight. The target was camouflaged to the seaward side, which hampered the reconnaissance somewhat – but also indicated that the target was of some importance to the enemy.

When darkness fell and before the moon rose too high, the two canoeists were ready in their folboats to be floated off in the usual way. They had with them eight charges of plastic high explosive, packed in bullet-proof and water-proof bags, each weighing 28 lb. It was vitally important to make a thorough job of this demolition at the first attempt. There would be no second chance if the first attempt failed or only partially succeeded, once the element of surprise had been lost. Tug Wilson fully realised this and paid the greatest possible attention to detail in his preparations, in order to ensure bringing off a really big and effective bang.

He was keyed up, but evidently very cool and calm, judging from the fact that, after he had paddled to the beach, landed successfully and unloaded the bags of explosives one at a time, he glanced back towards the submarine and, reckoning that she was too near the shore and too visible for safety, calmly paddled back on his own and suggested to the captain that he should withdraw to a more discreet distance.

Quite unruffled by this slight adjustment, the two commandos made their way cautiously up a steep embankment, with their tommy-guns at the ready, to reconnoitre more closely the large bridge that was to be their target. They were relieved to find it unguarded, but it was clearly a very solid structure. They made four journeys back and forth to carry their explosives from the beach.

The bridge was, as hoped, a railway-bridge spanning a deep ravine, built on concrete pillars with steel girders. It was to the latter that Tug proposed to attach his charges. This called for a combination of monkey-like agility and a rock-climber's strength – both of which attributes Tug's wiry frame possessed. He could climb like a monkey and hang with one hand, leaving the other free for fixing his charges in position. This was attributable to his abnormal power-weight ratio – with his power proving quite remarkable for a man of his size.

When the eight charges had been carefully fixed in place, with four of them on either side of the bridge, they were connected with cordtex. Then they were all inter-connected by an instantaneous fuse.

Finally a lead was attached hanging down towards the beach, which was lit as a slow fuse. The two men ran.

They just had time to hurtle down the bank and reach the beach – but not to dodge the hail of debris falling on to the beach and into the sea. However, they and their canoe were intact and silently and swiftly they made their way out to the waiting form of *Utmost*. The canoe was now lightened by the removal of the heavy bags of explosive, and their spirits were high with the knowledge that they had just brought off their third and biggest explosion, which had been fully successful beyond all doubt.

This demolition in the Gulf of Taranto perhaps marked the high-water mark of their wave of sabotage success for Tug Wilson and Marine Hughes in that eventful summer of 1941. Obviously the Italians weren't going to sit back and endure these dagger-thrusts without tightening-up the guarding of their coasts and the defence of vital strategic structures.

But Tug Wilson and Marine Hughes remained keen for further success and were in *Utmost* on her next patrol, in September 1941. This time they elected to wreck the track in a large railway tunnel to the south of Naples. This was to be a really big explosion and for this purpose two canoes were used to ferry the extra supply of explosives. The two men landed on 22nd September. They made straight towards the tunnel, but this time, sure enough, they came upon an enemy patrol in the tunnel and were fired upon in the dark. They fired back, but were unable to lay their charges and were obliged to return to the submarine.

Undaunted, they landed the next night further down the coast, bent on demolishing a three-span bridge, just north of the Gulf of Santa Eufemia. For the second night running they found their chosen target guarded and were fired upon by a sentry on the bridge. This time it was a much closer shave for them and they only just made it back to *Utmost* which had to make a very hurried dive out of danger. Things were hotting-up.

When Tug returned to Malta on 3rd October, he was called before Captain 'Shrimp' Simpson and told that, on instructions from higher up, his operations were now too dangerous and must cease forthwith. This was a great disappointment to Tug, but, while conceding that the position had now become difficult as a result of the three big explosions that he had brought off, he saw no reason why he shouldn't still be able to find and attack long unguarded stretches of railway-line – even if it had clearly become unsafe to attack tunnels and bridges. Besides, he had been giving the matter some thought and had devised a method of speeding things up. He could prepare his charges in readiness to lay against the lines just as a train was approaching – rather than have to attach fuses and detonators, which involved exposing himself for longer and running the risk of detection. Having set the Mediterranean ablaze, he was anxious to keep it glowing!

With 'Shrimp' Simpson's continued backing, he soon had another chance, in a hitherto unmolested area. On 18th October 1941 Tug was aboard a T class submarine, HM S/M *Truant*, under Lieutenant-Commander Hugh Rider Haggard, the tall (6ft 4 ins) thin grandson of the famous novelist of that name. *Truant* was a new submarine on its way from Barrow-in-Furness shipyard, via Gibraltar and Malta, to join Number 1 Submarine Flotilla in Alexandria. The idea now was for her to enter the Adriatic, by way of the Straits of Otranto, between Italy and Albania. Tug Wilson would thus have a chance of making his presence felt for the first time on the east coast of Italy – his previous landings having been on Sicily, the Gulf of Taranto and the west coast. There might still be an element of surprise left on the Adriatic side.

This was to prove a long and arduous patrol. Almost anything that can happen on a patrol seemed to overtake *Truant* on this last leg of her long journey from Barrow-in-Furness to Alexandria. Tug experienced a naval gun engagement, torpedo action, surface craft overhead and at one stage the submarine became stuck on the bottom of the ocean with only ten feet of water over her periscope. But despite all these problems, Tug for his part achieved a successful derailment of a train on the Adriatic coast, between Senigallia and Ancona. His new idea of clipping ready-prepared charges on to the rail when a train was approaching worked perfectly.

After a twenty-one day patrol Tug Wilson and Marine Hughes arrived back at Alexandria in November, having left it for Malta in April of that year. They arrived in *Truant*, with the gratifying sound of a successful explosion still ringing in their ears. They had enjoyed a good run of success with the Malta submarine flotilla and, in accordance with

Winston Churchill's express wishes, the Mediterranean had been set well and truly ablaze.

CHAPTER 7

# Limpets and Agents

On arrival at Alexandria, on his second wedding anniversary, 17th November 1941, Tug Wilson was welcomed ashore by Roger Courtney at the Special Boat Section's base aboard HMS *Medway*. He was greeted with the news that his captaincy had come through, and Roger Courtney had every intention of helping him celebrate this well-earned promotion, coupled with his wedding anniversary.

When this had been suitably attended to, a new scheme was afoot. Tug Wilson and Roger Courtney had devised a new way of affixing limpets to the hulls of ships, three at a time in a special frame, thereby multiplying their penetrating power with a more concentrated blast. The Special Boat Section had already scored a success with limpets in Benghazi harbour, when a merchant ship had been holed and sunk. Unfortunately the two members of the Special Boat Section who had carried out this coup, Sergeant Allan and Marine Miles, were captured after their canoe hit a jagged rock. They went 'into the bag' as prisoners-of-war.

Armed with his new limpet device, Tug Wilson was summoned to appear with Captain (S) Raw, the commander of Number 1 Submarine Flotilla, in front of Admiral Cunningham, the Commander of the Mediterranean Fleet. Tug was very enthusiastic over his new gadget and confidently demonstrated its use by affixing it to the bulk-head of the Admiral's cabin. He did so with the nonchalance of youth, whereas Captain Raw sat somewhat to attention on the edge of his chair in the presence of the Admiral. The latter's comment was: 'Fine – but rather you than me!'

Arrangements were soon made for the team of Tug Wilson and Marine Hughes to sail in HM S/M *Torbay*, under Lieutenant-Commander Anthony Miers, who had already had recent experience of conveying Commandos. *Torbay*, in company with *Talisman*, had on her previous patrol carried the Commando force which had attacked Rommel's headquarters at Beda Littoria. Miers was a tough and

Second-Lieutenant Robert Wilson, Royal Artillery, in 1939.

Marjorie Wilson in 1946.

determined extrovert. He was very keen never to miss a chance of action and was later awarded the VC and DSO and Bar.

On 4th December 1941, *Torbay* conveyed Tug Wilson and Marine Hughes to the western shores of Greece, with the intention of trying out the new limpet gadget. The harbour of Navarino was the area of choice. Wilson and Hughes slipped round the boom, into the harbour but, despite a thorough search, couldn't find a target to which to attach their limpets. After paddling for a very long time – far too long for the liking of Anthony Miers, who had been sitting waiting for them for about two hours in his submarine in a very tricky spot – the canoeists were obliged to return to the submarine without trying out their limpet-mines.

On the night of 21st December a target was found – an enemy destroyer lying off Navarino pier. Tug paddled to within a hundred and fifty yards of the ship and getting into the water started to swim with his limpet-frame in front of him. Despite wearing 'long-johns' as a protection against the cold, he found the temperature of the Mediterranean on this mid-winter night far colder than he had expected. With a modern wet-suit he would have made it to the ship but, despite determined efforts to defeat the cold and reach his target, he had to be pulled back, by a rope attached to him, with teeth chattering and hands numb, by his partner Marine Hughes. Disappointing though it was to have to return with the new limpet gadget still untried for the present, after getting so near and yet so far, to continue would have proved suicidal and also unsuccessful. Tug was almost at the end of his tether.

Early in the new year, he was sent back to Malta, this time without his trusted partner Marine Hughes. He travelled on the surface, in a merchant ship, feeling very exposed. After travelling far and wide underwater in submarines, he found it a strange and by no means reassuring feeling to be on the surface once more. This apprehensive feeling was only increased when an escort destroyer was torpedoed and sunk one day out of Alexandria.

Tug was glad to be back among his friends in 10 Submarine Flotilla on Malta. 1941/1942 was indeed Malta's blackest period, but the spirit of everyone, servicemen and civilians alike, was nothing short of marvellous. Social life, although difficult, was much of the time hilarious. For Tug, when off-duty, the routine was to have dinner in the mess before going ashore to his friends to join them for the evening. Submariners were on special rations – and few would begrudge them that – whilst the civilians were perforce on meagre fare, as were members of the other two Services. On occasions Tug would invite an Army friend along for a pre-lunch drink and a meal in the wardroom. The guest's comment would be: 'Do you mean I can have this *or* that?' People on Malta had become unaccustomed to being offered a choice.

By 12th January 1942, Tug was back in *Urge*, his mission this time being to land an agent on the Tunisian coast – explosions being temporarily in abeyance. What sounded rather a tame assignment compared with his previous landings and demolitions, turned out to be far from easy for Tug. He was asked to land an agent of considerable standing and of Middle-Eastern appearance, complete with a radio with which to signal vital shipping information back to base. Whereas the tide in the Mediterranean in most areas varies little, and consequently the surf is usually not turbulent, the sea off the North African coast is much more tidal, with breakers to contend with.

Having selected a beach for landing, Tug paddled in to shore with his agent aboard the canoe, clasping his precious radio. They came in on the crest of a wave, but in no time found themselves capsized. The force of the wave luckily carried them onwards to the shore. The fact that the agent was now soaked through could have proved fatal, because he was due to board a train in order to reach his destination, and would have looked highly suspicious in dripping clothes. By a lucky coincidence it was pouring uncharacteristically with rain and his wet state didn't make him much different from anyone else he might encounter. Nor did the immersion of his radio prevent it from performing sterling work later.

But for Tug there now arose the problem of paddling his way back to *Urge*, through the strong surf that had already capsized him on the way in. The manoeuvre proved tricky and exhausting, and it was only at the third attempt that he reached the open sea – and safety. It was a close call.

Despite the soaking and near-drowning that he suffered, Tug's morale was soon restored, when he arrived back at base in Malta to be greeted with the good news that, for his deeds of valour, he had been awarded the DSO – a somewhat exceptional decoration for an officer of his rank. This very point was noted in a letter that he later received from his old employer with the Bristol Aeroplane Company. The Managing Director, Sir Stanley White Bt, wrote to congratulate Tug Wilson on his award of the DSO in the following words:

19th May 1942

Dear Captain Wilson,

It is a great pleasure to me to offer my personal congratulations, and the congratulations of all with whom you were associated whilst working with this Company, upon your being awarded the DSO. What this decoration implies when awarded to an officer of Captain's rank we fully recognise, and we all feel proud that a former member of our staff should have merited such a distinction.

I have no doubt that in the days ahead, before the war has been finally won, you will continue to act with the same fearlessness and steadfastness to duty, and that you may emerge from the conflict with safety and with even added honours is my most sincere desire.

Yours sincerely,
G. Stanley White.

The award was duly celebrated in the most appropriate place possible – the wardroom of the submarine base at Lazaretto, from where most of Tug Wilson's exploits had started.

Now Tug Wilson was called home to the United Kingdom. He was sent for by 'Shrimp' Simpson and asked if he was willing to undertake an urgent mission on his way. Two important agents needed to be landed near Carthage. This would be Tug's ninth exploit by submarine (excluding his short abortive trip in *Urge*, when the Captain got lumbago). He accepted without hesitation.

The submarine this time was to be HM S/M *Upholder*, which had the largest tally of sunk enemy shipping to her name, under the skilful handling of the legendary Captain, Lieutenant-Commander David Wanklyn, VC, DSO and two bars. Her total amount of enemy shipping sunk was 125,000 tons in the space of sixteen months – including three U-boats, one destroyer, and a 17,800 ton troopship (the *Conte Rosso*), plus two cruisers and another destroyer hit. David Wanklyn was known, perhaps inevitably, as 'Wanks' and Tug knew him well from meetings in the wardroom at Lazaretto base and had a tremendous admiration for him. He was six feet two inches tall and bearded. He had a striking presence and a distinguished bearing, as well as a record that had earned him the loyalty and respect of his crew. Tug felt honoured to be travelling with such a renowned captain and crew.

Wanklyn had originally asked to return to the Adriatic, where he and his crew had had good hunting. But 'Shrimp' Simpson reckoned that his recent sinking of a German U-boat entering Brindisi had been highly dangerous and accordingly sent Wanklyn and *Upholder* in the opposite direction.

The idea was that first the two agents should be landed near Carthage and that then *Upholder* should rendezvous at a given point in the Mediterranean, enabling Tug to move over with his canoe to *Unbeaten*, which was commanded by Lieutenant-Commander Teddy Woodward, on her way to Gibraltar for repairs. Thus Tug would be on his way to the United Kingdom, intending to complete his journey somehow from Gibraltar.

All went well with the landing of the two agents. With the lesson recently learned off Tunisia, with regard to the rougher surf to be encountered on that coast, Tug decided that an inflatable RAF rubber dinghy must be used this time (despite the noise made in inflating it) for the two agents, who would be towed to the edge of the surf by Tug in his canoe. The two agents were duly landed and this time Tug had no difficulty in paddling back to the submarine.

Now *Upholder* had to make her rendezvous with *Unbeaten* off the island of Lampedusa, between Tunisia and Malta. By the time that the two submarines reached the appointed position, by night, the sea had become decidedly choppy – so much so that Wanklyn gave Tug the option of transferring, despite the rough sea, or remaining with *Upholder* and returning in her to base, to wait alternative transport to Gibraltar. It was up to Tug.

He didn't hesitate in making what was to prove a most fateful decision. He elected to make the change-over and head for Gibraltar – and for home, taking with him a spare battery and other requested equipment for *Unbeaten*.

As Tug neared *Unbeaten* the Number One's voice called out, by way of encouragement: 'Piss off, Tug. We've got two feet of water in the fore-ends and the batteries are gassing. You'll never make it to Gib.' Undeterred by this badinage, Tug went safely aboard *Unbeaten* – unwittingly the wisest move he ever made because, shortly after this, *Upholder* was tragically lost with all hands. Tug had, of course, been the last person to see David Wanklyn alive.

As for the Number One's remark to Tug as he neared *Unbeaten*'s conning-tower, the joke proved almost prophetic. She was indeed in a bad way and had to complete the final day's voyage into Gibraltar on the surface – luckily without mishap. Fortune favoured her and she arrived safely.

Tug Wilson had thus completed an eventful first leg of his long journey home, by the end of April 1942 – and in so doing had had a remarkable personal escape from death, which had so tragically overtaken the captain and crew of *Upholder*.

# CHAPTER 8

# 'This Side Up - Definitely'

Tug Wilson spent a week in transit in Gibraltar, oblivious of the fact that he had escaped death in *Upholder* by a whisker. He was due to fly home to Britain, but gave up his seat to a more urgent passenger. Instead of flying, he was sent onwards in a corvette, named HMS *Gardenia*. The journey took ten days, through submarine-infested waters, which called for all the manoeuvrability for which corvettes are renowned.

After docking at Liverpool, which had been extensively bombed but was still operating as a port, he went down to Bristol for a short visit to his wife, whom he hadn't seen for sixteen months. Marjorie had been working, while he was away, for the Ministry of Works, mainly in connection with Bailey bridges, which were to play such a vital role when the Allies eventually moved to the attack. He found her in good health and spirits, despite her inevitable anxiety over him and the frequent bombing raids to which Bristol had been subjected.

Very soon Tug had to report to the Flag Officer Submarines, Admiral Sir Max Horton, at Northways, Swiss Cottage. The meeting consisted of a gin and a chat. First Tug received congratulations on his achievements and his recent decoration. He was also told how lucky he was to be alive and that the two North African agents whom he had landed were doing sterling work by sending back most valuable information. Then came the grim news of David Wanklyn and the crew of *Upholder*. As the last man who had been with them, Tug was asked for full details of the patrol, up to the time of his transfer to *Unbeaten*. Tug was deeply shocked but was glad to be able to hand over a recent photograph of 'Wanks' for the Admiral to send on to his widow.

Tug's next visit was to Ardrossan, on the west coast of Scotland, facing the Isle of Arran, where he rejoined Roger Courtney, who had come back to the United Kingdom in order to form Number 2 Special Boat Section, leaving Major M. R. B. Kealy, of the Devonshire

Regiment, in charge of Number 1 Section, with fifteen officers and forty-five other ranks under him in Alexandria.

Tug had been chosen for a new experimental role in submarine/canoe warfare. He went first down to London to collect his DSO at Buckingham Palace and then to Hertfordshire, where he was taken by car to what was enigmatically known as Station 9. This place was so secret that it was jokingly said that even the transport drivers had to be blindfolded for the last mile of the journey to it!

This was the Inter-Services Research Bureau, at The Frythe, Welwyn, where an extraordinary variety of secret war-gadgets were being developed and tried out, with the help of such inventive characters as Sir Malcolm Campbell. Tug's particular gadget was to be a mini-torpedo, 21 inches long, to be fired at close range at enemy shipping from a canoe, operating out of a submarine. The torpedo had a hollow-cavity charge of plastic high explosive, in order to achieve a maximum effect from a minimum size. It was, propelled by a modified windscreen-wiper motor, with twin opposed propellers to keep it in a straight line. It also had a hydrostatic depth-finding device. The torpedo was powered by special batteries and was started by pressing a button. There was a white line down its back, visible under the water, to indicate its course. After some hurried preparations and tests, Tug was sent to try it out in earnest. But first he had to get himself and his torpedoes into the right war-zone to carry out this important experiment.

Finally he was booked to fly out to the Middle East by flying-boat from Poole Harbour in Dorset. He made the journey in civilian clothes, armed with a personal letter from Lord Louis Mountbatten, Chief of Combined Operations, in case there should be any difficulty with His Majesty's Customs, over the strange appearance of the accompanying luggage, or at any later time on his journey – and quite a journey it turned out to be!

He departed early on 7th August 1942 from the Inter-Services Research bureau, north of London, by car to Victoria, and caught the British Airways special pullman for Poole. On arrival, the four boxes, marked: 'THIS SIDE UP - DEFINITELY', aroused a certain amount of curiosity on the part of the Customs and difficulties began to arise. Tug refused to allow the firmly screwed-down lids to be removed and asked to see the Customs Security Officer, hoping that the latter had been briefed in the matter. A telephone call from the Customs Security Officer to Combined Operations Headquarters did the trick, and the boxes were allowed through unopened.

After some hours of waiting, the passengers were informed that the flying-boat would not be leaving that day. Tug's boxes were taken over by the Customs Security Officer and safely stowed away. All the passengers were taken by road to Bournemouth.

Two days later, on 9th August 1942, they eventually took off aboard the huge British Airways flying-boat, the Golden Hind. The overall time taken and the stops of varying duration that had to be made on suitable stretches of water, under wartime conditions, nowadays seem incredible. But after starting their journey on 9th August, it wasn't until 17th August that they reached Lagos, in Nigeria. They travelled via Foynes, in the River Shannon in Western Ireland, Lisbon, and Bathurst on the Gambia.

From Lagos they changed planes and made for Cairo, landing at Kano and Maiduguri, in northern and eastern Nigeria respectively, Fort Lamy in Chad, Khartoum in the Sudan, Wadi Halfa on the frontier between the Sudan and Egypt on the Nile, and finally to their destination at Cairo.

On arrival at Cairo, on 21st August 1942, Tug Wilson immediately contacted Combined Operations at General Headquarters by telephone and requested a naval car to collect himself and his gear. Interviewed by Admiral Maund at Combined Operations Headquarters, he explained the nature of his mission and produced Lord Mountbatten's covering letter. He was ordered to present himself to the Commander-in-Chief, Mediterranean Fleet, in person.

Two days later he was on his way by road, in a naval car, with one of his four boxes and was presented to Admiral Harwood, the Commander-in-Chief of the Mediterranean Fleet. The Admiral was very interested in the possibilities of the proposed experimental operation, after Tug had revealed the contents of the box and had explained the functions and capabilities of the new weapon to the Admiral and two of his staff. He was asked in which enemy harbour in the Mediterranean he would like to carry out the operation. Tug specified Navarino, where the cold had defeated him on a previous exploit with limpets. He was told that he could choose between Numbers 1 and 10 Submarine Flotillas for his starting-point  –

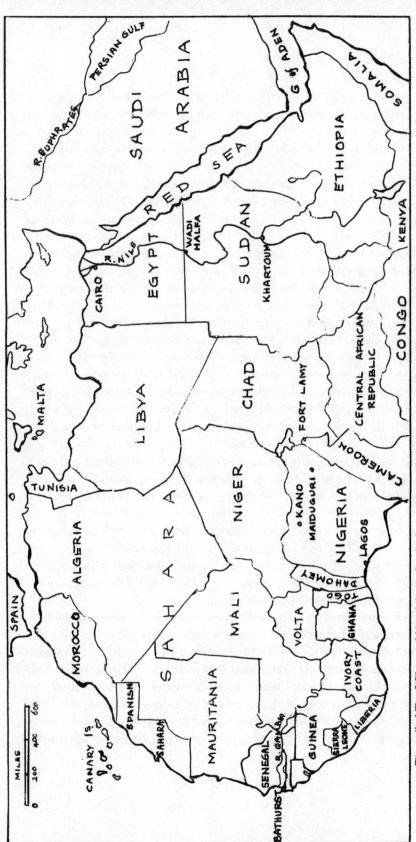

The trail of Tug Wilson and his mini-torpedoes in August 1942. The journey was made in a Sunderland flying-boat from Poole (in Dorset), via Foynes (Ireland), Lisbon (Portugal), Bathurst (Gambia) to Lagos (Nigeria). Thence the journey was continued by transport planes via Kano and Maiduguri (Nigeria), Fort Lamy (Chad), Khartoum and Wadi Halfa (Sudan), Cairo (Egypt) and finally to Malta. The circuitous journey took eighteen days.

Alexandria or Malta. The choice fell on Malta, whence Tug's most successful sorties had been made. He returned to Cairo late that evening.

One thing that struck Tug about Cairo at this time was the comparative emptiness of the place. When he was there in 1941 one almost had to fight one's way through the crush to the bar in Shepheard's Hotel. Gone now were the hordes of 'Gabardine swine' (as front-line troops tended to call the desk-bound staff-officers in Cairo). Gone too were the parties of mixed tennis at the Gezira Club. Monty's arrival had much to do with this – after his preliminary joke about Rommel being halted by weight of numbers at Gezira.

The next thing was for Tug to get himself and his mini-torpedoes to Malta with all speed. He went to Movement Control (Air) in the morning and requested a passage to Malta, emphasizing his urgency and producing documentary evidence in support of his claim – there being a long priority list of people waiting for transport. He was eventually given a chit and told to proceed to an aerodrome some twenty miles out of Cairo. Having acquired the necessary transport to get there, Tug presented himself at the aerodrome to a squadron leader who, after hearing his story, assured him that he would get him away that evening to Malta.

There were two other passengers aboard the aircraft: Lord Gort and his ADC, Lord Munster. This was Tug's second meeting with Lord Gort, whom he had met during his short stay at Gibraltar earlier in the year en route for Britain. As Governor of Gibraltar, Lord Gort had wanted first-hand information on conditions on the beleaguered island of Malta. Lord Gort was on his way there now in connection with the award of the George Cross that the gallant island had received earlier in the year. They travelled in a Douglas DC3 by night, with Tug sleeping on the mail-bags in the cargo space.

Early next morning, on 25th August 1942, the plane landed on Malta. After breakfasting at the airport, Tug was taken to the submarine base at Lazaretto. The wardroom stewards were already up and about and, after recovering from their surprise at seeing Tug once again, they kindly offered him a cup of tea. After an early-morning swim to refresh him, followed by a shower and a shave, Tug wandered round the cabins, looking for old familiar faces of friends dragging themselves reluctantly out of bed. He eventually found himself outside the cabin of Captain (S), 'Shrimp' Simpson, who was just having his morning cup of tea. Tug ventured in. 'Shrimp' grinned broadly, on his entry, and on hearing of the purpose of his return, roared with laughter, in typical manner.

It was nearly five months since Tug had left Lazaretto and there were many new faces in the wardroom, with very few of the old submariners left – no 'Wanks' Wanklyn; no 'Tommo' Tomkinson; and no Dick Cayley. In ways it was all strangely different, and of course inevitably sad, but Tug found that these men in 'the trade' (as submariners referred to their daring profession) were all of a certain stamp, and very soon, when the bar opened and everyone was equipped with a glass in his hand, the atmosphere peculiar to 'Shrimp' Simpson's wardroom soon returned. Long before lunch it was like the old time and place, so beloved by those who, like Tug, had known it.

So, after a strange Odyssey from Poole to Malta, Tug Wilson had finally reached his destination – with his boxes still 'THIS SIDE UP – DEFINITELY'. He himself was ready and keen for further action.

# CHAPTER 9

# Mini-Torpedo Trial

On land, the end of August and the beginning of September 1942 marked the high water mark of Rommel's tide in the Middle East, which had at one time looked likely to carry him past Alexandria and Cairo to the vital Suez Canal. By mid-July after his victorious eastward advance, this time capturing Tobruk in June, along with thousands of prisoners-of-war and a considerable amount of stores, he had been held by the Eighth Army under General Auchinleck at El Alamein. Here the El Alamein line ran down at right angles from the coast nearly to the Qattara Depression, which was a vast area of soft sand and not considered passable by an army. At this point the distance between the sea and the Qattara Depression was at its shortest and thus the El Alamein line formed something of a bottle-neck and was therefore a suitable choice for a defensive stand to halt Rommel's Afrika Korps and their Italian allies. Futhermore, it was now Rommel who had to keep his forward troops supplied over a vast distance – a task which the Allies had found so difficult in previous months. Now the boot was on the other foot.

Early in August General Montgomery was flown out from England, at Churchill's insistence, to replace the unfortunate General Auchinleck who, after stabilising the fighting with the limited forces at his disposal, had to hand over to a successor at the very time when reinforcements in men and material were arriving in significant numbers. The new Grant and Sherman tanks were becoming available, to replace the Matildas and Valentines, and the hopelessly light Honeys, with which Auchinleck had had to make do.

August 31st 1942 found Rommel making what was to be his last advance towards Alexandria and Cairo. Montgomery, who now also had a growing air superiority to call upon, cunningly left an empty area between the southern flank of the El Alamein line and the Qattara Depression. He professed to prefer fighting his battles on ground of his own choosing. Rommel after making a feint frontal attack, largely with Italian troops, then obligingly poured his armour into this inviting gap, in a characteristic attempt to outflank the defences and strike up at them from the south – repeating the tactics that had served him so well earlier that summer with the Gazala line in Libya. This was just what Montgomery wanted to happen and it was the signal for repeated air-strikes from formations of Boston bombers, as well as for a counter-attack by the now strengthened Allied armour.

The result, within a couple of days, was a wholesale destruction of Rommel's tanks, which he could ill afford to lose – along with the recapture of large quantities of British bully-beef tins, with which the Germans had gratefully stocked their tanks after the fall of Tobruk. The no-man's-land to the south was littered with burned-out or immobilised German tanks.

By 3rd September, the remnants of Rommel's armour that had been committed to battle were obliged to withdraw to a point behind their side of the El Alamein line, whence they had set out. This battle of Alam Halfa was a decisive victory for Montgomery and an important boost for the Eighth Army.

Now the stage was set for a big build-up of forces by Montgomery, which was to culminate in the even more decisive battle of El Alamein, which began on the night of 23rd October. Meanwhile several behind-the-line attacks, by land and sea, were staged against Rommel's now over-stretched supply lines along the coast and elsewhere in the Mediterranean. The biggest of these took place on 14th September against the harbour of Tobruk, by land and by sea, in order to demolish the port installations and deny the use of the port to the Germans and Italians in the landing of reinforcements and supplies for their troops in Egypt. Though this raid doubtless had an unnerving effect on the rear defences of the enemy, it also resulted in heavy losses for the attackers – a large proportion of whom were captured after their destroyers had been sunk.

Also in September 1942, a Special Boat Section raiding-party, operating from Beirut, landed on the island of Rhodes, and did extensive damage on the strategic aerodromes at Marizza and Calato, before most of the raiders were captured.

Tug Wilson's experimental attack on shipping with his new mini-torpedoes was set to take place against a background of all these events – with every knife-thrust at the enemy's ports and harbours counting.

The U-class submarine earmarked for this operation was known as *P42*, later to be named *Unbroken*, under Lieutenant-Commander Alastair Mars (who ended up with a DSO, DSC and Bar to his name).

The operation was preceded by a meeting between Captain (S) 'Shrimp' Simpson, Mars and Tug Wilson. Whereas on all his previous escapades the choice of the precise place for a landing had been left to Tug Wilson and his submarine commander, without the foreknowledge of Malta, now for the first time Malta was to know where Tug was going for this important test. The reason for this departure from the normal custom was that up-to-date photographic reconnaissance by air was considered essential, in order to locate a suitable harbour. The harbour chosen was Crotone, on the advice of Captain 'Shrimp' Simpson, after a close study of several possibilities in Sicily and Italy.

Crotone is under the 'foot' of Italy, right under the ball of the big toe, on the east coast of Calabria, just north of the Gulf of Squillace. The reasons for the choice of Crotone may be summarised as follows:

(a)   As the operation was of an experimental nature, it was important to select a harbour from which there was a reasonable prospect of returning and reporting results.

(b)   As there was no minefield round the harbour, a close approach by the submarine was considered feasible – to within 2,000 to 3,000 yards.

(c)   The harbour was small and any ship lying at anchor was bound to do so in the deep water along the mole, not far from the harbour entrance – which favoured a quick getaway to the open sea by the attackers.

(d)   The harbour was not very busy and had sustained only one RAF raid, and had suffered no other molestation – not even from Tug Wilson!

(e)   During this raid, the southern mole had received a direct hit from a bomb and had been breached in one place down to sea level. This gap might prove useful.

(f)   Numerous recent aerial photographs were available, right up to the day of the submarine's departure, clearly revealing the boom.

(g)   Vessels up to 4,000 tons could be accommodated in the harbour, which would justify the experimental attack with the new mini-torpedoes.

For this operation, in the absence of Tug's regular partner, Marine Hughes, the choice had fallen upon Bombardier Brittlebank, a delightful quietly-spoken Englishman of very solid and powerful build, who as Lieutenant-Commander Mars observed 'would follow Tug to Hell and back'. Brittlebank had already proved his worth by surviving the raid on Rommel's headquarters and returning after a long trek on foot across the desert with Lieutenant-Colonel R. E. Laycock, in late 1941. Tug met him for the first time in Malta, and Brittlebank was delighted to be chosen as his partner. Mars described Tug Wilson as 'a slim wiry fellow, radiating confidence'. They were a well-blended partnership and all seemed set for a successful experiment.

*P42* left Malta on 31st August 1942 – just as Rommel's tanks were setting out on their final bid for a breakthrough to the Suez Canal.

A large part of the time on the outward voyage was spent by the two Commandos on cleaning and checking their considerable array of arms and equipment – somewhat to the amusement of the submarine's captain, Alastair Mars. They seemed to him to be for ever oiling, testing, polishing, sharpening, adjusting and generally fondling their weapons of war. He reckoned that they regarded sleeping and eating as unfortunate necessities – cruel partings from their cherished weaponry. But for Tug and Bombardier Brittlebank this preoccupation helped to pass the time, and left as little as possible to chance. It was doubtless this sort of attention to detail that led G. B. Courtney, younger brother of Roger, in his book *S.B.S. in World War II*, to describe Tug as '. . . . without doubt the most skilled and experienced railway saboteur in *SBS*.'

By 5th September *P42* was in position off Crotone to carry out a daylight periscope reconnaissance at a distance of about four miles. Sure enough a suitable target, a merchant ship of 2,000 to 3,000 tons was lying alongside the north mole of the harbour. The estimated time required for the completion of the whole operation was one-and-a-half to two hours. The moon wasn't expected to rise until 3 a.m. the next day and, since Lieutenant-Commander Mars was anxious to be on his way by that time, an 11. 30 p.m. start was decided upon.

As darkness fell, the submarine slowly drew closer to the harbour, and at 11.40 p.m. the folboat was silently launched, heavily laden, about 2,000 yards east of the harbour. Tug and Brittlebank continued on a compass bearing westwards towards the harbour entrance. Apart from a slight breeze and gentle swell, the sea was flat and calm, with a clear sky and good visibility. It looked like being a good night for the operation.

From 250 yards out, Tug sighted the seaward end of the south mole. Splitting paddles and using only one half, in order to make a quiet approach, with the minimum amount of phosphorescence stirred up, the two men cautiously approached the harbour entrance square on, so as to present a minimum silhouette. The boom across the harbour, though not impassable, raised a problem. Tug reckoned that, in view of its comparatively short length, if there were look-outs posted at the end of each mole, a craft however small would most certainly be spotted approaching from seaward.

Accordingly, Tug turned about and they made a wide detour to the south, in order to investigate the bomb-damaged south mole, and find out if the breach previously seen in the reconnaissance photograph would afford a safer way into the harbour – without their having to risk crossing the boom. They reached the breach in the mole and investigated. Barbed-wire and wire-netting had been stuffed somewhat haphazardly into the gap, which reached down to sea-level. It was possible to fold the wire upwards and leave room for the canoe to float through underneath the wire.

Having enlarged the gap, they had no difficulty in easing the canoe through. Their first obstacle had been safely cleared, and they were on their way in.

In the harbour itself all was calm and still – and deathly silent. The merchant ship could be seen lying alongside the northern mole, almost directly opposite the breach in the south mole, through which they had made their entry. The target was estimated at about a hundred yards in length and looked easy enough to hit. The ideal position from which to fire a mini-torpedo was at an angle of about fifty degrees – thereby allowing a good margin of error.

In order to reach this ideal position, Tug Wilson decided to take a course which kept the canoe as far away as possible from a schooner which was also at anchor in the harbour. While Brittlebank sat forward

Preparing for action from a folboat.

A folboat in motion.

using a single paddle, Tug was aft, ready with the torpedoes. They approached deliberately and carefully, anxious not to create any noise or phosphorescent glow.

All went well as they cautiously worked their way to their chosen firing position. Tug was checking his angle when the still silence was shattered by a raucous challenge from the schooner. This was immediately followed by a shout from the target ship. There was no time to lose and Tug removed the nose from one of the torpedoes and placed it in the water. He pressed the starter button and, as instructed, he gave the propeller a quarter turn and pressed the button a second time. To his relief the mechanism functioned perfectly and the motor started. It sounded in good order.

He warned Bombardier Brittlebank to stand by with his double-ended paddle in readiness for a quick getaway. With the torpedo just under the water, Tug took careful aim and released it, with a gentle push to help it on its way. He had done his bit – now it was up to the mini-torpedo to prove its worth.

Immediately he ordered Bombardier Brittlebank to paddle flat out, and soon grabbed his own paddle. He took a final glance at the disappearing torpedo and saw that the white line along its back was pointing directly at the target. In Tug's mind all was in order – all they needed now was a confirmatory bang to indicate a successful hit.

By now, following the sentry's challenge, a commotion had started and lights were appearing – though as yet no shots had been fired. With both canoeists now paddling hard, they soon reached their point of exit from the harbour, the breach through which they had sneaked in. Amid the commotion the two men listened hopefully for a big explosion – but in vain. Despite seeing the mini-torpedo well on its way to its target, there could be no guarantee of a hit. Perhaps the sound of the explosion had been muffled by the general uproar, but they couldn't be sure. Similarly, the captain listening on the submarine, some 3,000 yards away, heard bangs and saw flashes in the harbour, but was unable to confirm a definite explosion in the short time that he was able to listen.

The two Commandos emerged from the harbour and all they now had to do was paddle for 3,000 yards along a pre-arranged compass-bearing and find their waiting submarine. This was something that Tug had done many times before with little difficulty. In fact, on only one occasion had he previously had to use his torch with which he was provided. On every other occasion he had managed to sight the submarine without recourse to the pre-arranged signals by torch. This time there was a slight swell getting up and the horizon became gradually less distinct, but Tug was still confident.

After about half an hour's fruitless search, Tug sighted what looked like the familiar blob of a submarine on his port bow, and he turned hopefully towards it. A moment later he spotted a similar object to the port of the first. He soon realised that he had spotted two surface craft, approaching in line abreast. It was too late to do anything but pass between the two advancing vessels, which were moving at about ten knots, and hope for the best.

On the spur of the moment, but taking careful aim, he launched one of his three remaining torpedoes over the port side at one of the ships. It was a moving target but it seemed worth a try – abortive though it proved, as the bows of two dark and light-grey camouflaged vessels, possibly destroyers, loomed up one on either side of the folboat. Tug was ready to jettison his remaining mini-torpedoes, to prevent these secret weapons from falling intact into enemy hands. But this was unnecessary as the canoe seemed to have passed unnoticed between the two ships, which were doubtless patrolling with their attention focussed much further ahead. The folboat then had to survive the danger of capsizing as it passed between the two ships' wakes.

Tug realised that the submarine's Asdic would have picked up the hydrophonic effects of the two patrolling craft and would have been obliged to take evasive action. It now seemed certain that no hope remained of joining the *P42* that night. It was by then 1.45 a.m.

It was normal for an alternative rendezvous time and position to be arranged in case of emergency. Almost the last words of Lieutenant-Commander Alastair Mars to Tug, in confirmation of this, had been: 'If you fail to make the rendezvous because we've been chased away, steer due east to the dawn rendezvous five miles off the breakwater. If we don't meet there, continue due east and we'll be on that line.'

Unfortunately the weather was steadily worsening, and the two men found a considerable swell, with occasional white horses, running diagonally across the course towards the dawn rendezvous. The avoidance of capsizing required such concentration and effort that, by dawn there could be no certainty as to their exact position.

Furthermore, the canoe was now heavy with water which had inevitably been shipped during the buffeting that had been sustained. The compass and binoculars in the boat were too soaked to be of use. But as the sea calmed appreciably with the arrival of dawn, at least Crotone was visible in the right place. They couldn't be far out.

They remained in and around that position for two hours, keeping a sharp look-out all around them, but becoming more apprehensive by the minute. As a final resort, Tug decided to explode two four-second hand grenades, in a desperate effort to attract *P42*'s attention, in case she had dived in the vicinity for safety reasons. Before throwing the grenades astern, they paddled at maximum speed in order to be well clear of the explosions.

When this last card had been played to no avail, Tug and Brittlebank could now only assume that *P42*'s captain had not considered it advisable to remain on the surface, for very good reasons not known to the two unfortunate canoeists.

The state of the canoe was now such that it urgently needed beaching for baling-out and, if possible, repairing. They paddled south of Crotone, round Cape Colonne and searched for a suitable beach for landing. They soon found one that appeared to be approachable only from the sea, being surrounded by high cliffs. This secluded position would enable them to attend to their canoe unmolested. But before they rowed towards it, the two remaining torpedoes must be jettisoned, to prevent them from falling into enemy hands. At a point nearly two miles out to sea they were flooded and sunk.

After landing and baling, it was evident that the canoe was by no means in a sound state, but after they had spent twenty minutes patching her up she was ready to float once more. They lost no time in putting into operation the only plan of escape that now seemed open to them. They pushed off from the shore and began the daunting prospect of paddling their way to Malta – a distance of two hundred and forty miles. Bombardier Brittlebank had gallantly found his way back across the Libyan desert, following the raid on Rommel's headquarters at the end of 1941, and now he didn't flinch from the prospect of another long haul to safety. Tug intended to hug the coast of Calabria, and then that of Sicily, before striking across the open sea to Malta. At least they had eight days' food with them, and they were both men of proven determination.

First, they set course across the Gulf of Squillace. They passed a few fishing boats and were hailed at a distance. In return they waved back. There was no sign of any uniformed seach parties in these boats, which was a relief. But by 6 p.m. the state of the canoe had become so parlous that there was no alternative but to make for the shore. This time it wasn't possible to select a secluded beach – in fact they were fortunate to reach land without sinking.

This time they felt sure that they had been observed landing. The game was up and Tug's luck had finally run out.

# CHAPTER 10

# 'Whacko, you Pommy bastard!'

The two weary canoeists reached the shore and dragged themselves and their leaking folboat up a sloping beach to some bushes growing in the sand beyond the shingle. They hid the canoe as best they could from view in the bushes. The two Commandos then sat down on the beach and rested for a while, to recover from their strenuous exertions which had taken their toll. Apart from the short break during their earlier landing, to empty and repair the canoe before setting out to paddle to Malta, they had been in the folboat for a total of eighteen hours. They needed to gather their strength.

Bombardier Brittlebank lay prostrate while Tug Wilson was sitting wondering what options, if any, were now open to them – stranded as they were on the mainland of Italy with a leaky canoe and all contact with their submarine lost. He didn't have long to ponder. Suddenly over the crest of a hill behind him he heard excited voices. Looking round he saw a posse of Italian soldiers rushing down the hill towards him, yelling something that sounded like '*Mani in alto!*' (Hands up!). The game was obviously up and all Tug and Bombardier Brittlebank could do, under all the circumstances, was to comply with these urgent and unmistakable instructions.

As Tug had feared, they had indeed been seen approaching this beach and in very quick time the local Carabinieri had been informed. Tug Wilson and Brittlebank were wearing khaki-drill with cap-comforters of the type favoured by the Commandos on their heads. They were caught red-handed, but at least they were in British army uniform, which ought to prevent their being shot as spies. But they realised that they would be closely interrogated about the events of the previous evening in Crotone harbour – not to mention a whole series of other explosions in Southern Italy.

Their immediate worry was to calm their triumphant but strangely jittery and trigger-happy captors. The officer in charge was shaking like a leaf – whether from fury, indignation or sheer fright, it was hard to tell. For the present they were much more interested in Wilson and Brittlebank than in the canoe. Tug and Brittlebank were not allowed anywhere near the latter, and were bundled off in a truck that was waiting over the brow of the hill. They were closely guarded by the Carabinieri, with guns and pistols at the ready, still quivering with excitement. The situation remained tense.

The two Commandos were driven to a Carabinieri barracks a few miles inland and, as they journeyed apprehensively along, they had time to ponder their immediate future. Like most newly-taken prisoners-of-war, they hadn't given much previous thought to the matter. Such thoughts were morbid and bad for morale – besides, it probably wouldn't ever happen to them! Of one thing they were certain: they would only divulge their name, rank and army number, in accordance with instructions based on the Geneva Convention concerning the interrogation of prisoners.

On arrival at the barracks they were led into an office, on the wall of which were large photographs of Hitler and Mussolini side by side. Tug was unable to refrain from pointing to them and exclaiming in English, 'What an unholy alliance!' This remark, which appeared to be understood, brought no rebuke. The two prisoners were put into separate cells.

Soon the inevitable time arrived for searching, and the procedure was nothing if not thorough. In turn and separately they were stripped stark naked. Then followed a most intensive and intimate search, which was really rather a formality, because their few belongings were in the canoe. They were given some pasta, which they devoured ravenously and were left for the night in their cells, under close guard. So far there had been nothing to complain of in their treatment – but they still wondered what the morrow would bring.

The morrow brought an immediate transfer by truck to an army barracks in Catanzaro, a larger town than Crotone in the Gulf of Squillace. Here they were brought separately in front of a high-ranking Italian army officer who interrogated them in English. He was, under the circumstances, remarkably pleasant to Tug – though he punctuated the interrogation with: 'Of course I could shoot you!' What really puzzled him was how on earth a British army officer came to be fighting the war from canoes and submarines? He made rather half-hearted attempts to persuade Tug to give details beyond the obligatory name, rank and number, by explaining that, if only he could be supplied with more information, then Tug's next-of-kin could be told without delay that he was safe and well – and a prisoner-of-war. Tug didn't fall for this line of persuasion and the matter was eventually dropped, and the interview petered out.

With Bombardier Brittlebank a less subtle and more intimidatory approach was adopted. He was told quite simply that he was to be shot. Equally simply he replied that, in that case, he would like to be allowed to write a last letter to his next-of-kin. His resigned reply caused a bit of a stir, but no notepaper was produced.

Here the matter rested. Not that the two Commandos knew about it, but it was only a month later that the notorious Hitler Order concerning the 'extermination' of 'so-called Commandos' was published – on 18th October 1942. Whether this order would have applied to Commandos captured by Italian troops on Italian soil was very doubtful – but it most certainly was applied in several cases of Commandos caught in Norway around this time and subsequently.

Tug and Bombardier Brittlebank were prepared to take what was coming to them. They had volunteered for this hazardous work and it was no use moaning and having second thoughts now. They were both quite fatalistic about the matter.

After two days at Catanzaro, during which they received reasonable treatment, with three more repetitive interrogations, conducted separately, to break the monotony and keep them guessing as to their ultimate fate, they were eventually put on a train for Naples, under heavy escort. It struck Tug as a trifle ironic that he should now be travelling in reasonable comfort, in a second-class carriage, along the very same coastal railway that he had spent much of the previous summer sabotaging.

As recently as the previous month he had been in England, about to leave on his circuitous journey by flying-boat to Lagos and thence across the northern half of Africa to Cairo and on to Malta. He had succeeded in firing one of the mini-torpedoes at a stationary target in Crotone harbour and was confident that he had set it well and truly on its course. Beyond that, he couldn't be sure.

Besides wondering in vain what had been the outcome of his firing of the torpedo inside the harbour of Crotone, he also inevitably found himself wondering, equally in vain, what had prevented the submarine from keeping its rendezvous and picking them up. It was indeed puzzling, after completing nine previous re-entries on other occasions without any hitch. But no amount of pondering would alter his present predicament. This in turn led to thoughts of home and his wife, Marjorie. Would he ever see her again – or she him, for that matter? Thoughts of this nature kept rushing through his mind as the train took him on his way to an uncertain fate.

After travelling steadily for most of the day, the train pulled into a large station at Naples. It was evidently the evening rush-hour, judging by the swarms of Italian civilians milling around. Tug and Brittlebank had to change platforms in order to board a train for Rome, they were told by their escort. Their appearance caused quite a stir and a menacing crowd of onlookers gathered round them. It was a relief to be installed in a second-class carriage once more.

They journeyed through the night and reached Rome early next morning. On arrival they were taken by truck to a cavalry barracks, where they were put into separate cells. Tug was able to look out of the window and his spirits rose when he saw some very un-Italian men playing football on a parade-ground. At first he thought they might be British prisoners-of-war, but soon learned that the barracks was used by German troops on leave in Rome.

Six days later, without further interrogations, Wilson and Brittlebank were put once more on to a train. This time the train headed eastwards over the Appenines until, still up among the hills, they came to a station marked Sulmona, near which there was a prisoner-of-war camp for officers and for other ranks, in separate compounds. Once again Tug and Bombardier Brittlebank were split up, but at least they were still in the same camp – and what was more, in was an ordinary prisoner-of-war camp, which indicated that, much to their relief, they were to be regarded as ordinary prisoners-of-war, despite the clandestine circumstances of their capture.

When Tug Wilson was brought by his escort before the camp commandant, the latter fixed a rather distasteful gaze on him before rounding on him sharply because his namesake, Woodrow Wilson, had given Italy such a rotten deal after World War I (in which Italy had fought on the Allied side, he stressed). All Tug could do was to shrug his shoulders.

Then he was marched off to the officers' compound. As the sentry unlocked the gate to let him in, Tug was stopped in his tracks by a shout of: 'Whacko, you Pommy bastard! How are you? Good to see you.'

Tug had undoubtedly arrived at a prisoner-of-war camp – and an unmistakably Australian one, at that!

# CHAPTER 11

# Sulmona Sortie

Tug discovered that he was in Campo di Concentramento 78, at Sulmona. This had been one of the earliest prisoner-of-war camps to be established in Italy and was predominantly populated by Australians. Whereas prisoners-of-war in Germany were mostly grouped into camps according to what Service they were in, with separate camps for the Royal Navy, Merchant Navy, Royal Air Force and Army, with nationalities sometimes mixed, as at Colditz for instance, in Italy the Services were mostly intermingled, while the nationalities were mainly segregated. Thus Australians were usually sent to one particular camp, which was Sulmona, while New Zealanders and South Africans were concentrated at Modena. There were, of course, many exceptions to the general rule.

The purpose behind this segregation of Dominion and Commonwealth troops from those from Britain was doubtless the vain hope that the 'Colonials' could be weaned away from the mother country, if kept away from British influence. In the event, the Italian authorities could hardly have been wider of the mark. They had reckoned without the extremely staunch support that the Commonwealth forces had given to the common cause against Hitler and Mussolini. They turned out to be, if anything, even more steadfastly pro-British than the British themselves, as far as the Italians were concerned – as the Germans also found when they tried unsuccessfully to form Irish battalions to fight for them.

Thus some camps in Germany tended to offer their reluctant inmates a certain amount of variety by virtue of the many nationalities to be found in some of them, whereas those in Italy tended to achieve interest from the fact that members of all Services were liable to be assembled within one camp. Thus Tug, much of whose service had been with the Royal Navy, now found himself with representatives of all the Services and their sub-divisions, which he found stimulating.

At that time at Sulmona the Aussies were in the majority, with over two hundred officers there, when Tug arrived, compared with about a hundred and fifty British. Though the Australians were housed in separate huts, the two nationalities were able to mix within the compound. Despite jocular remarks about 'Pommy bastards' on the one hand, and 'Aborigines' on the other, they all got on well enough. The Pommies learned to say 'Whacko!' (whatever it might mean) by way of a friendly greeting.

Tug Wilson and Bombardier Brittlebank were not the first Commandos to reach Sulmona. As early as February 1941 thirty-five men of X Troop of Number 2 Commando, including their leader, Major T. A. G. Pritchard, had been parachuted into southern Italy to blow up an aqueduct over the River Tragino, near Calitri, some sixty miles inland to the east of Salerno. Their rescue rendezvous, very optimistically arranged and never reached, was to have been with a submarine at the mouth of the River Sele, south of Salerno. Despite bold attempts, after successfully blowing up the important aqueduct, to struggle over the high mountains in winter, they were all rounded up and captured. With the exception of one unfortunate parachutist, who was of Italian birth and therefore regarded as a traitor and shot, they were nearly all sent to Sulmona.

Of these Commando paratroops, Captain Christopher Lea and Lieutenant Anthony Deane-Drummond (later a Major-General) had managed to escape over the wire but were recaptured. Lea was wounded, but recovered and after the war ultimately became a judge. Deane-Drummond made a second attempt, successful this time, and brought off the remarkable achievement of the first 'home run' (via Switzerland) made by a prisoner-of-war in Italy.

This comparative dearth of 'home runs' from Italy, compared with the creditable total notched up from camps in Germany, was attributable to several factors. In Germany, there were so many foreign workers in strange garb and of varied appearance, both in the towns and countryside, that an escaped prisoner-of-war stood a reasonable chance of passing himself off as a foreign worker. He still needed forged papers to stand a good chance of success, and the crossing of the various frontiers still presented a formidable obstacle which few could overcome.

But in Italy, an escaping Anglo-Saxon stood out among the populace like a sore thumb. The best he could hope for was to be taken for a German deserter. Furthermore, contrary to what might be imagined from the enormous number of Italian civilians and peasant farmers who helped escaping Allied fugitives and ex-prisoners-of-war after the September 1943 armistice, prior to that date the Italian populace was very patriotic and observant. They were exceedingly quick to alert the local Carabinieri to the presence of any suspicious strangers in their midst, thus making it extremely difficult for escaped prisoners to get anywhere after escaping, which in itself was by no means easy from Italian camps.

Whereas an escaper in Germany had a choice of possible nationalities to assume, if stopped and questioned, in Italy there was little hope of anyone with a fair complexion passing himself off as an Italian, and there were no foreign workers with whom to merge.

Another limiting factor was the drawback that many of the Italian prisoner-of-war camps were situated in central or southern Italy and, failing the remote chance of finding and stealing a suitable boat on the coast, the way up Italy to Switzerland was long and fraught with hazards to be surmounted – all of which makes Deane-Drummond's successful escape the more praiseworthy.

None of these factors, however, deterred the more dedicated escapers among the prisoners-of-war from constantly devising escape plans, which had to be approved by the prisoners' escape committee, which was set up in each camp in order to prevent uncoordinated efforts from clashing – thus resulting in well-conceived plans being ruined by some spur-of-the-moment hair-brained scheme upsetting everything.

In Sulmona Tug Wilson met a fellow prisoner who was a kindred spirit as far as escaping was concerned, Guy Greville by name, a captain in the Royal Tank Regiment, who had been captured early in September 1942, when his Valentine tank was put out of action during a skirmish with Rommel's panzers in front of the El Alamein line. He was a Supplementary Reserve officer, commissioned into the Royal Tank Corps before the war. He came from a family with a long military tradition in India and had himself been fortuitously born in Burma, because his mother, when seven months pregnant, elected to accompany her husband on a military mission in that remote country. Pre-natal Guy was evidently in a hurry to see the light of day and promptly did so in the hills of Burma. Now in Sulmona it seemed that he was in a similar hurry to emerge. He had been an active tunneller from the start.

When Tug Wilson met him at Sulmona, he had been working on a tunnel that was discovered by the Italians, who were adept at spotting these things, aided in some cases, it was thought, by the use of stool-pigeons infiltrated among the prisoners. Guy was of similar size and the same age as Tug, both of them being in their late twenties when the war had started. They were now thirty and married, and Guy had three children at home. They had long and earnest discussions about finding a way out of Sulmona camp and were both intent on escaping somehow.

Then one day in June 1943 Tug received a note from his folboat partner, Bombardier Brittlebank, from the other ranks' compound, saying that a working-party would be going outside the compound and that this might possibly offer a chance of escaping. The officers' compound was on a higher level than that of the other ranks. A barbed wire fence on top of a wall against a bank separated the two compounds. By day the wire fence was covered by two high sentry-boxes, one at either end, and a transfer from one compound to the other was out of the question. But by night, if one chose one's moment when the lights were beamed elsewhere, it would be possible to get through the barbed wire fence and drop down into the other ranks' compound below.

It was decided that Guy Greville who, like Tug, was light, agile and fearless, should drop down into the lower compound, and that an other rank, organised by Brittlebank, should be hoisted up to replace him, in order to keep the figures right at roll-call. Guy Greville duly contacted Bombardier Brittlebank and waited for three days until a working-party was announced for the following day. He sent a message to Tug and after dark the necessary change-over was made to the other ranks' compound. With Tug and Guy reunited in the other ranks' compound, all was now set for the working-party next day.

The task of the working-party was to load up wood on to a hand-cart and deliver it to the camp kitchens. There were two enormous piles of wood and the prisoners were in no hurry to complete the task. By early afternoon enough wood had been transported and when the work was nearing an end, Tug and Guy quickly disappeared into the wood, one in each pile. The other members of the party covered them over with branches, pretending to be working on the piles. On their return to the compound there was no check on numbers, since they hadn't been outside the main camp perimeter.

The two escapers had to remain for several more hours in very cramped and uncomfortable positions under the wood, not daring to move. It was an enormous relief when darkness fell and finally it was safe to crawl out of their hiding-places. Tug freed himself without much difficulty, but Guy was stuck fast. The other prisoners had heaped a lot of wood on top of him, in order to make sure of concealing him. It was a nasty moment for him, but luckily Tug was able to come to his rescue.

They were now free and outside the prisoners' compound, but they still had to get beyond the high perimeter fence which encircled the whole camp, including the Italian soldiers' quarters. They crawled cautiously to the outer fence and decided that their best bet was to burrow under it. They had no wire-cutters and to attempt to climb over it would be far too risky. It was much safer to keep down low, well out of sight. Luckily the fence had been erected in sandy soil and they were able to scoop it away to a sufficient depth to allow them to crawl under and away out of sight. What was more, they were able to replace the earth, thus covering their tracks, in case an observant sentry came on his rounds later.

In the dark they crawled noiselessly away until they were out of range of the camp lighting. They hoped to make for the Adriatic coast and look for a boat which might get them across to Yugoslavia – or, failing that to board a goods train to the north, towards the Swiss border. For this purpose they had each been issued with a supply of lire, which the camp escape committee kept available for escape plans that had their blessing. The source of this money was not divulged, but it reached most camps by one means or another. The two escapers also had some Italian-type civilian clothes over their army uniform.

Their immediate objective was to put as much distance as possible between themselves and the camp by dawn, when they would hide up somewhere. Their progress was slowed by heavy going across country, mainly over agricultural land. It was also hot, even at night, at that time of the year, which was mid-June 1943. The night was short and dawn was all too soon upon them, and they had yet to come upon any likely cover among trees. The country was all so open. When it was almost light, they found some rather isolated and scraggy trees and had to make do with these for cover.

Soon after dawn the surrounding fields seemed to fill with Italian peasant-workers. The two escapers lay low but kept a look-out. Nobody approached them but, judging from too-frequent glances in their direction, their half-hidden presence had been spotted. They could only lie low and hope for the best. At about mid-morning a group of armed Carabinieri was seen advancing across the field, making straight for the spot where Tug and Guy were lying. The Carabinieri spread out and surrounded the two escapers, before closing in on them with rifles cocked. They were distinctly menacing and hostile. At that stage of the war, Mussolini was still in power and Italian soldiers and police were still keen on doing their duty – in some cases very officiously.

Wilson and Greville were bundled into a truck and taken back to Campo 78 at Sulmona and brought before the commandant. He tried in vain to find out their method of escape, but it soon became clear that the replaced earth hadn't yet been found. Tug and Guy certainly weren't letting on and it was several days before their exit place was discovered.

The two officers received the maximum sentence allowed by the Geneva Convention to be imposed on prisoners-of-war for escaping – thirty days of solitary confinement. They were led off to the 'cooler' and were fortunately incarcerated together in the same cell, which was considerably preferable to solitary confinement. Another blessing was that, far from going hungry, they received better rations than they were accustomed to, because the British orderlies responsible for bringing them their food saw to it that the escapers got more than their normal ration, plus some tobacco with which to roll themselves some cigarettes.

Even so it was a relief when the thirty days were over and they were returned to the officers' compound. It hadn't developed into a epic escape, but it had been a commendable break-out which was to stand them both in good stead in the near future. It had also earned them the official label of '*Pericolosi*' – dangerous ones, who were usually sent to the 'bad boys'' Campo Cinque, in a rocky fortress at Gavi, near Genoa.

Whatever the outcome, this escape had served to whet their appetites for further freedom.

CHAPTER 12

# Bologna Blunder

Two days later Tug Wilson and Guy Greville bade farewell to their friends in Sulmona and left with two camp guards as escort to an undisclosed destination. They were put into a second class carriage, which they shared with their guards, on a train that headed north from Sulmona. It wasn't long before they extracted from the guards the information that they were not bound for the punishment camp near Genoa, as expected, but for a brand new camp at Bologna. This was interesting, and possibly encouraging news for them to ponder.

In view of the fact that they had only just emerged from the cooler at Sulmona, and had not yet had a chance to build up their reserves of energy or escape rations, they decided against making a break in transit, unless a really inviting opportunity presented itself. With Sicily now invaded and already in Allied hands, it seemed highly likely that an invasion of mainland Italy would soon follow, and that it would be wiser to await events and see what life at Bologna had in store for them. The big snag, however, was that they were being moved further north and therefore further away from any impending Allied landing in the south. But at least they were not going as far north as Genoa.

On arrival at Bologna, they were marched from the station for a short distance to the northern outskirts of the city, to Campo Concentramento Per Prigionieri di Guerra N.19, to give it its full name. They waited at the main heavy wooden entrance gates to be let in. On either side of the gates were high walls of buildings which housed the camp guards and administrative staff. The two new arrivals were escorted along a passage into the presence of the camp commandant, whose name was Aldo Magagnoli – a fact that they subsequently gleaned from his signature on the camp paper currency, valid only for use within the camp, and pretty valueless even there, for the simple reason that there was nothing to buy, apart from a limited amount of low grade vino.

81

THE MONASTERY, PADULA

*An unconventional POW Camp in Southern Italy. Campo P.G. 35 housed an interesting assortment of Allied POW's in the Padula monastery in World War 2.*

Evidently their notoriety as escapers had preceded them, because the commandant warned them, through an interpreter, against trying to escape from his custody at Bologna. He added that, as they had already served their month's incarceration for escaping at Sulmona, they would be allowed to join their comrades in the main camp, to which they were now led.

In order to get there, they had to walk eighty yards along a tarmac road between two high barbed-wire fences, at the end of which were the gates, also of barbed-wire, into the main prisoners' compound.

As Tug and Guy entered the compound, they found that they were in a large rectangular space, flanked on either side by one-storey barracks, with tiled roofs and cement-block walls. There were six of these long low buildings on either side, and the two newcomers were led into the second on the left and shown to two vacant iron beds with mattresses on which they dumped their few worldly goods.

The entrance to each building faced inwards towards the central rectangle, where prisoners could walk up and down for exercise – an occupation with which some were currently engaged, in preparation for the walking that they might well have to do over the Italian hills. On entering each barrack, there was a central passageway with three or four bays, each holding a dozen beds, with windows at the end, on either side of the main passage. At the far end of the passageway were swinging doors leading to the ablution section of the building, with wash-basins and hole-in-the-floor lavatories, where precarious squatting on two foot-rests was the method required. All in all, the accommodation was rather better that most prisoners-of-war had been used to.

Bologna camp had in fact been recently constructed as a barracks for Italy's militiamen, but had been turned into a prisoner-of-war camp instead. There was a cookhouse at the end of the compound, beyond the furthest sleeping quarters, and there was one building set aside for feeding.

The camp was surrounded by a high wall, with barbed wire on top, and there were sentries in watch-towers at the four corners. As the land was flat, little could be seen of the immediate surroundings of the camp, though some of the taller buildings in the city were visible in the distance.

Tug Wilson and Guy Greville were soon among former fellow-prisoners, and one reunion in particular was destined to prove of great importance in the near future. One day in the 'mess', while eating his 'skilly', Guy Greville spotted across the table a pre-war friend of his – Sherard Veasey by name. Recognition was rather slow at first, because Sherard had grown a beard, rather than continually having to borrow other people's shaving-kit. He had only recently been captured and hadn't yet received a next-of-kin parcel from home, with shaving-kit and other vital necessities. As there were other beards on view in the camp, mostly licensed growths belonging to naval officers, he decided to let his grow until a razor of his own arrived from home.

Sherard Veasey had known Guy Greville in London, but in 1935 had left to join the Palestine Police and after completing his contract for a three-year stint he had returned to England in 1938. The outbreak of World War II found him working as a management trainee with Marks and Spencer at their Hull branch. He immediately joined up in the nearest infantry regiment, the Duke of Wellington's, and was soon sent to Sandhurst OCTU and then commissioned in the Worcestershire Regiment and posted to a battalion engaged on coastal defence in Yorkshire. Almost at once he volunteered to serve in the newly formed Commandos and was sent to join 4 Commando in Scotland for some very strenuous training, in September 1940.

Veasey's action with 4 Commando included participation in the first Lofoten Islands raid, off Narvik in northern Norway in March 1941 under Lieutenant-Colonel Dudley Lister, MC, the Boulogne reconnaissance raid under Lord Lovat, DSO, MC, in April 1942, and the Dieppe raid in August 1942, again under Lord Lovat. In May 1943 he was sent on draft to the Mediterranean to join 3 Commando under Lieutenant-Colonel John Durnford-Slater DSO, only to be torpedoed en route in a troopship which sank off the North African coast near Derna. He was picked up by a corvette of the Royal Australian Navy and reached 3 Commando at Port Tewfik on the Suez Canal in the nick of time to sail with them back westwards for the July invasion of Sicily.

There he took part in two landings – the first near Cassibile, south of Syracuse, being unopposed, but the second by no means so. Fighting their way three nights later through the coastal defences at Agnone, the men of 3 Commando hurried inland to capture the Malati bridge near Lentini, behind the enemy lines on the road north to Catania.

This action was a classic example of the use of shock troops and the bridge was later re-named by General Montgomery 'The Commando Bridge', in honour of their achievement and of his appreciation. Unfortunately for Sherard Veasey, after the task had been successfully accomplished, while attempting to link up with the main body of conventional troops, whose advance had been delayed by the untimely arrival of the Hermann Goering Parachute Regiment, he was captured by the latter. He was handed over to the Italians for custody and taken to the mainland and sent to a transit camp at Capua, near Naples, and thence to Bologna. He was thus one of the newest prisoners – with less than a month 'in the bag' when he met his old friend Guy Greville at Bologna, in August 1943.

With Guy Greville and Tug Wilson having one joint escape to their credit, and a yearning for another taste of freedom uppermost in their minds, it wasn't long before plans were being discussed, with Sherard Veasey included in the conversation. Meanwhile Bologna camp was rapidly increasing its number of inmates, from camps further to the south. First, the Australians, plus a few British officers, arrived from Sulmona, and a batch of mainly British prisoners arrived from Chieti. But by far the largest contingent, five hundred in all, arrived from Padula, which was a camp in a monastery, right down in the south of Italy, in the hills to the south of Salerno. Their arrival brought the total number of prisoners now gathered together in Bologna to close on a thousand.

Padula Camp, in the unusual setting of a monastery, contained a very wide spectrum of mainly British prisoners-of-war – most Australians having been concentrated at Sulmona, and South Africans and New Zealanders at Modena. At Padula, prisoners had been gathered together from all three Services: Royal Navy, Army and RAF, with some fairly outlandish branches of all three included, thus making it a most interesting camp. For instance, there were representatives from the Special Boat Service, in which Tug Wilson had fought, the Long Range Desert Group, SOE, SAS, and a surprisingly large haul from the Army Chaplain Corps. The presence of the last of these was a reflexion of the fluid nature of Desert warfare, especially with Rommel around. The same reason also accounted for the presence of an elderly ordnance expert, whose seemingly safe job it had been to examine captured pieces of enemy ordnance. But in what was later known as 'the Gazala Gallop' in June 1942, after one of Rommel's lightning advances across the Desert, it was the ordnance expert, and not the enemy ordnance, that was captured!

From the Royal Navy, submariners from the underwater battle in the Mediterranean, as well as those engaged in surface activities, were to be found – as were several Royal Marines who had been deposited in the sea off Tobruk from the destroyer HMS *Sikh* on September 14th, 1942. Some of them had been obliged to take off their boots, in order to keep afloat, and had been captured ashore without them. The next pair of boots that they wore came six months later, when they reached Padula and were issued with Red Cross army boots on their arrival from Bari transit camp. Until that happy day, they had to make do with the bottoms of date boxes tied under the soles of their feet, like primitive sandals.

From the Army there were representatives from most of the most famous cavalry regiments, who had been put into light, under-gunned tanks, with disastrous results as soon as Rommel's Afrika Korps arrived on the scene. There were also gunners and infantrymen who had gone into the bag as a result of encirclement by Rommel's fast-moving spearheads, dating back to his appearance in Tripolitania to bolster up his Italian allies and push back the British and Commonwealth troops to the Suez Canal and if possible capture it. If one talked to a fellow prisoner-of-war, it was highly likely that he would explain that he had been captured by the Germans (which there was little reason to doubt) and almost immediately handed over to the Italians for custody. One also gained the impression that of these prisoners, more than half had been captured by the ubiquitous 90th Light Division, who had a habit of turning up when least expected or wanted. Padula also housed several British officers serving with the 4th Indian Division, who had born the brunt of much of the Desert fighting in command of Indian troops. Even some members of the Army Dental Corps had managed to get themselves surrounded and captured – to the considerable advantage of the teeth of their fellow-prisoners. There was one Harley Street practitioner and other skilled dentists among them, and although dental materials were in short supply, many patients never had better attention before or after.

The RAF contributed a cheerful assortment of shot-down officers who had survived, including a handful of Canadians, who introduced a type of modified baseball to camp life. Some had been shot down or forced to land behind the enemy lines; others were the survivors of the continual battle for Malta, from where Germans convoys supplying Rommel could be attacked, or British shipping in the Mediterranean needed to be protected – with heavy losses in fighter pilots. The Fleet Air Arm, too, was represented.

As one might expect from such a wide spectrum of prisoners, a very resourceful collection of talent and enterprise was gathered together in the monastery at Padula. Some of the earlier prisoners had known bad times as well as good. In the early days in the winter of 1941/1942, when Red Cross parcels didn't seem able to make their way intact on their journey down Italy, and the war news seemed to go from bad to worse, when Leningrad was besieged, Moscow threatened and Hong Kong and Singapore taken, and Allied losses in shipping and planes were first multiplied and then broadcast over the camp loud-speakers to unwilling ears, morale was hard to maintain on empty stomachs. The fall of Tobruk in June 1942 didn't help much either. But from the late summer of that year, beginning with the halting of Rommel in Egypt, his repulse at Alam Halfa and his reverse and retreat at the Battle of El Alamein, coupled with the halting of the Germans by the Russians at Stalingrad, leading to the eventual turn of the tide on the Eastern front, the outlook improved dramatically and morale was boosted. But to the inmates of Padula, something dearer to their hearts, or at least to their empty stomachs, began to happen. Thanks to the persuasive efforts of one of the Italian speakers among the prisoners and a co-operative entrepreneur among the Italian interpreting staff, co-inciding with the long awaited steady supply of Red Cross parcels, a very active black market was set up, to the mutual advantage of prisoners and interpreters alike. Cigarettes were the key to the trade that ensued, aided by genuine coffee from Red Cross parcels, by now virtually non-existent in wartime Italy, as a profitable alternative. Out went cigarettes and coffee, and in came a variety of local farm produce, usually camouflaged in whicker baskets, hidden under supplies of fruit and tomatoes, which were allowed to be bought with camp currency. In this way eggs, meat and, most tempting of all, small barrels of condensed milk (every POW's favourite) made their way into the camp. On one occasion the meat arrived on the hoof, in the form of a couple of piglets, which were quickly ushered into the cookhouse.

It was marvellous while it lasted, but it was too marvellous to last for long. Someone blew the gaff and investigators were sent from Naples. In consequence, Padula lost one officer-interpreter and the Italian contingent on the Russian front gained one very reluctant reinforcement! However, during the boom, most prisoners had managed to regain a lot of lost weight and had been allowed to build up tin-stores against probable hard times to come. Some even had enough tins, and enough generosity, to slip an occasional present of food (never an easy thing for a prisoner-of-war who has known hunger) to an incoming prisoner sent to Padula after the black market had ended, and after a lean period elsewhere.

Before leaving Padula and returning to the arrival of its inmates at Bologna, there is one story which doesn't seem to have appeared in print before and may perhaps be worth recording. The accommodation for the prisoners was according to rank. On the two longest sides of the quadrangle there were small monastery gardens, with doors leading into them, through vacated monks' quarters. In these quarters the more senior officers, including two brigadiers, were housed. All other officers of lower degree were housed up above the cloisters, in the wings that ran along both sides and one end of the monastery quadrangle. British orderlies occupied some wooden huts within the quad and the Italian guards were quartered in the buildings of the forecourt, as well a few presumably evicted monks. One of the latter, Friar Tuck by nickname because of his dimensions, used to frequent the prisoners' precincts and wish anyone who hadn't taken advance evasive action a very unctuous *Buon giorno*. The forecourt also contained a 'cooler' for those who had escaped and been recaptured – including George Millar, of 'Horned Pigeon' fame, who later managed to escape from Germany and emerged as a very active organiser with the French Maquis in 1944, behind the enemy lines. Finally there was a field at the far end of the quadrangle, on to which the prisoners were allowed by day for exercise, and hereby hangs a tale.

The field had once been used for growing lucerne and the surrounding edges still yielded an abundant crop. What better way to use the lucerne than to cycle it through some rabbits, which could be kept on almost free range in one of the monastery gardens? So reasoned a certain flying officer, who had an affinity with rabbits, which in no way rendered him averse to the prospect of eating them when hungry. Someone remarked, possibly rather unkindly, that he even looked rather like one! Be that as it may, he had little difficulty in spiriting two bucks and five does via the camp black market into one of the monastery gardens, where he supplied them with daily bundles of lucerne garnered from the field. Getting them into the monastery was one thing, but getting them to multiply proved quite another. They seemed healthy enough but monk-like when it came to reproduction. But even if the flying officer's rabbits weren't fertile, at least his own imagination was. His mind turned to Red Cross special medical parcels. So he reported to the sick-bay and asked for a tin of Bemax – not for himself, but for his backward buck rabbits. This worked wonders. The rabbits bred and bred, until the rabbit score moved by the end of July 1943 from seven to two hundred and seven. That was how, when the camp was hurriedly moved to Bologna, after the Allied invasion of Sicily, the prisoners' last meal was a very tasty and filling fricassée of Padula rabbit, provided by courtesy of the RAF.

By the time this assorted collection of prisoners-of-war from Padula, Capua, Chieti, Sulmona and elsewere had been assembled at Bologna, by the first week of August 1943, the stage was set for dramatic events to unfurl. Already the writing was on the wall as far as Italy's continuance in the war was concerned. The dictatorship of Mussolini had come to an end when, on July 25th, he was deposed and arrested. Marshal Badoglio was now at the head of a government which was rumoured to be anxious to negotiate for Italian withdrawal from the war. It seemed that, following the fall of Sicily, the Allied forces were poised to strike at mainland Italy, and that there would not be long to wait before further action took place.

In the new camp an end of term atmosphere prevailed – though nobody could name the actual breaking-up day.

Thoughts of freedom loomed large in the minds of all, as the hot Italian summer blazed relentlessly down from a clear blue sky. There seemed little point in trying to escape now, with delivery quite probably at hand. But on the other hand it was obviously prudent to prepare for a possible trek over the hills to reach the Allied forces, wherever they might land.

To this end, most prisoners tried to save a little food from their Red Cross parcels for any future journey. Many tried to concoct some form of nourishing escape cake, from sugar, cocoa, condensed milk, wholemeal biscuits reinforced with calcium, and maybe some raisins if available. The result was a very concentrated slab – the prisoner-of-war's answer to an Everest climber's pemmican. Prisoners-of-war tended, not surprisingly, to be obsessed with food and its preparation and there was one classic case of two prisoners hard at work, side by side. One had received a Red Cross parcel containing a tin of porridge and was bent on converting it into biscuits. His companion had found a tin of oatmeal service biscuits in his parcel and was pounding away in order to make them into porridge – to the amusement of some interested onlookers.

Prisoners also gathered together their precious belongings and made themselves some sort of container for their essentials. Included among these essentials were, in some cases, a means of brewing-up tea – a legacy from their days in the parched desert, no doubt, when no halt was complete without quickly brewing-up some tea. Prisoners grew very adept at making tea on miniature portable stoves (locally known as *stufas*) made from tins from Red Cross parcels, on which a cup of water could be coaxed to the boil, with a little blowing, using a couple of twigs as fuel. To carry their belongings, those who had been captured complete with their haversacks were all right, but others had to improvise. A useful and comfortable carrier could be made by sewing up the tails of an army shirt, issued by the Red Cross, and tying the sleeves round one's shoulders.

Tug Wilson had his preparations well in hand for an emergency break-out, should it be necessary, and was determined to seize his chance when it came. He had been in the bag for nearly a year, but had remained reasonably fit and was determined to get home to his wife and back to active service. The bag was no place for a keen soldier, waiting and watching the war and promotion pass him by. At least Tug had had a good run for his money – unlike many of his contemporaries who had been captured in France in 1940. Nor were his conditions anything like those of prisoners now in the hands of the Japanese – though the full horror of what they had to endure only became realised when the war ended abruptly, with the lives of those who had managed to survive thus far saved in the nick of time by the dropping of two atomic bombs. Now, like Guy Greville, Sherard Veasey and the rest of his companions, he felt that he hadn't long to wait and that he must be patient for a little longer. To attempt an escape now would be inopportune and foolhardy, with all the attendant risks and dangers involved. He decided to wait.

He didn't have long to wait, for on 3rd September news was received over the Italian radio that Allied forces had landed in Calabria, at the extreme foot of Italy. A collapse of Italian resistance now seemed distinctly on the cards, judging by rumours that found their way from various sources into the camp. Now the prisoners waited impatiently for confirmation of landings further up the Italian coast. There was certainly a wide selection of rumours to choose from. These included a naval bombardment of the Italian naval base at La Spezia, well north of Rome, on the west coast of Italy, accompanied by a landing of Allied troops at Livorno nearby. These attacks were linked with a rumoured landing on the other side of Italy, on the Adriatic coast at Rimini, which was a mere sixty miles from Bologna. Prisoners were usually optimistic – it didn't pay not to be – and they were constantly poring over maps of the various war fronts. The more they studied the map of Italy, the more obvious it seemed that the Allies wouldn't bother to start at the toe of Italy and then work their way laboriously up the leg of this peculiarly shaped country. By landings from amphibious craft surely they would lop off great chunks of Italy, liberating prisoner-of-war camps as they went. It was small wonder that rumours of landings, albeit unconfirmed, were able to circulate so freely among the prisoners. But they had reckoned without the stubborn determination of the Germans to continue fighting from one well-defended position to the next, and the rugged nature of the Appenines which run almost the entire length of the country. Still less were they aware of the fact that after the capture of Tripolitania and Tunisia, and the whole of the north coast of Africa, there had been strong opposition on the part of the Americans to an assault on the Axis powers via Italy. A frontal attack on Germany, across the English Channel and through France, was favoured, in order to satisfy the insistent demands of the Russians. It was only Churchill's own insistence that carried the day and enabled the invasion of Sicily and Italy to go ahead, albeit on a less grand scale than he would have liked. Already thoughts and planning were turning to the second front elsewhere.

When 8th September 1943 dawned, the prisoners of Bologna camp knew nothing of this. Their minds were taken up with their own immediate prospects. Suddenly, these took a sharp turn for the better when, soon after 4 p.m., the Senior British Officer, a brigadier, was sent for by the Italian commandant. He was told that Marshal Badoglio had signed an armistice with the Allies and that as a result Italy was now ceasing hostilities. In the light of this the commandant was withdrawing his sentries and handing over control of the prisoners to the Senior British Officer. The latter enquired about the presence of German troops in the vicinity and the danger to his officers from that quarter. He was told that the commandant knew of none in the immediate area, but that in the event of any news of Germans arriving, a bugle alarm would immediately be sounded.

The Senior British Officer returned to the compound, where he found a large throng of prisoners anxiously waiting for news of his summons to the camp commandant. What he was about to tell them, when a general assembly had been gathered together, was to astound them and linger in their memories for the rest of their lives.

He reported on his meeting with the Italian commandant, giving the news of the armistice, and sure enough there were no longer any guards to be seen round the camp perimeter. And then came the bombshell!

Before the assembled prisoners had had time to assimilate his utterance and wax euphoric, he issued clear and measured instructions that for the present they were all to remain in camp, in accordance with secret orders received direct from England, until further arrangements were made by Allied forces. By way of emphasis and warning he added, in clear unequivocal terms, that anyone who disobeyed this order could expect to face a court martial. The words he chose left no room for doubt or choice. To his stunned audience he added by way of reassurance that he had arranged with the commandant that, in the event of any move by the Germans to take over the camp, an alarm would be sounded on a bugle. It was now early evening and he advised them to go to bed that night prepared to march out at short notice, should any alarm be raised.

The prisoners were baffled – just as they were in other camps throughout Italy. What they didn't know, and in many cases only found out years later, was that it was General Montgomery who was behind this puzzling and, as it turned out, disastrous order.

When Monty was appointed to command the invasion of Italy, he, like many other people on both sides of the camp barbed-wire, was under the illusion that the Italian campaign would be fluid and Allied progress rapid. One thing that he particularly didn't want was hordes of released prisoners roaming around the countryside behind the enemy lines, causing administrative problems and even indulging in well-meaning acts of free-lance sabotage against the enemy and, in the process, quite possibly blowing up bridges and installations that the Allies were counting on capturing intact. Under no circumstances would there be any question of dropping arms to prison camps.

Monty liked to conduct his campaigns in accordance with his own careful planning, on ground of his own choosing – as he had so often repeated to huge audiences of officers and men that he was in the habit of convening to hear his theories. He had started this custom as far back as 1941, when he was commanding XXX Corps in Kent, and had carried the practice with him to the Egyptian Desert – with great success, backed up by no little help from the advent of Sherman tanks and other battle-winning equipment, to coincide with his own arrival.

These instructions were issued at Monty's instigation via MI9, the organisation which was responsible for escape-lines and contact with prisoner-of-war camps in Italy and Germany, mainly by means of coded letters. These instructions reached camps throughout Italy in July and early August 1943, in time for the impending invasion, and the fact that they were of recent origin tended to convince any doubting Senior British Officers in the camps that they were very much in force and should therefore be transmitted to the prisoners at the appropriate time and duly enforced. There were a few Senior British Officers elsewhere who decided that local circumstances had changed since the orders had been issued and that it was now their duty to act accordingly and disregard them. The prisoners in those camps at least had a chance of escape, whereas those in Bologna, with a few exceptions, had none.

What Monty had failed to foresee, perhaps not surprisingly, was the swiftness and efficiency with which the Germans, far from withdrawing now that Italy had given up the fight as their ally, would rapidly pump in more troops to plug the gap, and that the campaign would last for another twenty months, rather than the twenty days that some optimists predicted.

Knowing nothing of all this, the puzzled prisoners took stock of their situation. The orders and the threat of a court martial were patently clear, and to men who had been trained to obey superior commands, these seemed definite enough. After all, the bugle alarm should give them time to break out if the worst came to the worst. Furthermore, life in a prisoner-of-war camp, though requiring a lot of resource and adjustment to the varying conditions, does not, however, attune people to decision making. Most decisions are made for the prisoners and there isn't usually much that they can do to alter them.

Now, facing a vital decision, the vast majority opted for the disciplined course of staying put as ordered. There were, however, a handful of independent spirits who decided to walk out while the going was good. Those who were observed doing so drew a mixed reaction from those who had chosen the course of discipline, some of whom expressed their disapproval and predicted dire consequences; others, who had nearly done likewise (but not quite), had a sneaking admiration for their effrontery and wished them luck. This admiration grew in intensity, and became tinged with envy, when news filtered through months later that some of them had reached safety in Switzerland – with never a murmur of disciplinary action.

Tug Wilson, who was imbued with the spirit of army discipline, despite his free-thinking exploits with the Special Boat Section of the Commandos, felt that he must obey the explicit orders and stay in camp with the rest. But he was in a state of readiness for a quick getaway if the alarm sounded.

These thoughts were uppermost in people's minds throughout the camp as they retired to their sleeping quarters. Most decided to sleep fully clothed, in many cases with their boots on and haversacks within reach, ready packed. Sleep was slow to descend on many of them amid the tension, but most had managed to drop off eventually from sheer exhaustion.

Then, suddenly, at about 4 a.m., just before dawn, a bugle sounded loud and clear – and with a note of urgency.

The Bologna blunder was about to become a disaster!

CHAPTER 13

# A Prisoner Vanishes

At the sound of the alarm bugle there was a rush from the barracks
of the main compound. The gates to the road leading to the main
entrance had been left unlocked, and the first wave of prisoners opened
them and surged three or four abreast along the road, between the
two high barbed-wire fences, followed by dozens of others.

When those in front had come to within thirty yards of the main
entrance, the high gates were opened and, as they peered through
the dim light of early dawn, to their consternation the huge form of
a tank appeared, barring their way ahead. They halted in their tracks
and, as they saw the long barrel of the tank's gun being lowered in
their direction, they flung themselves to the ground, in the hope that
the inevitable stream of bullets would pass over their prostrate bodies.

There was a deathly hush – but no shots followed. The massive
tank remained where it was, menacing and motionless. Gradually
those towards the rear began to melt away into the semi-darkness and
word was passed to the front that there was still a chance of escape
via the back gate at the far corner. Hurriedly those at the front retraced
their steps, back between the high barbed-wire fences flanking the
road, thus finding themselves now in the rear of a surge towards the
back gate at the far corner of the camp, beyond the last bungalow.
The milling scene was reminiscent of a disturbed ants' nest, with
prisoners running in several directions, carrying assorted bundles.
One officer, loth to be parted from his precious possessions, was seen
humping a trunk on his back!

Something like a hundred prisoners poured out of the rear gate
of the camp, on to a road that ran along the entire length of the
enclosure. At this moment machine-gun fire was heard, and those
in the road dashed to the far side, where there was some rough ground
with trees and bushes on it, bordered by a sparse but thorny hedge.
Three escapers were hit by bullets, one of them fatally, as it transpired.
In their desperation to get off the road and into cover, many prisoners

95

sustained scratches and tore their clothes as they groped their way through the hedge to safety and temporary refuge.

What had happened was that, besides barring the main entrance, another truck had been positioned at the front corner of the camp, thus covering the road that ran down the side. It was no longer safe to leave the camp by the back gate and emerge on to the road. Soon the Germans who had come to take over the camp, ceased firing and drove down the road to close the rear gate. With the bulk of their prisoners thus safely contained within the camp, in the nick of time, as daylight came German infantry soldiers began to comb the undergrowth in the adjoining wood, with fixed bayonets and rifles at the ready.

Some of the prisoners managed to hide themselves in the wood, which only covered a small area, with another road beyond it on the far side. Some reached a house and even spoke to the startled female occupant in their search for somewhere to hide. One who succeeded in making himself scarce – if not particularly savoury – burrowed into a pile of manure and thus escaped the attention of the Germans. The others were nearly all winkled out and brought back to the camp throughout the morning. For them the game was up. It had been hectic while it lasted!

As daylight arrived at the camp, so did some German guards, under the command of an officer dressed in a black uniform. He announced that his detachment of parachutists had been brought into the area with orders to take over the camp, which he had succeeded in doing pretty effectively.

For the prisoners it was a bitter blow to their hopes of freedom. In a short space of time all they had achieved by staying put was a change of custodians, from Italians to Germans – apart from a total of twenty officers who had escaped, including those who had defiantly and wisely walked out the previous evening. The situation, recently so rosy, now looked bleak indeed. The air was full of recrimination.

However, such is the inborn optimism of most prisoners-of-war that some were soon clutching at straws. Perhaps the Germans were just there to guard them before withdrawing their troops from Italy? Surely the Allied invasion forces would soon arrive to prevent them from being removed to Germany – the fate that was really uppermost in everybody's mind?

Gibraltar 1942. Captain R. Wilson, DSO, (centre), with (left) Lieutenant-Commander E. Woodward, Captain of H.M.S/M Unbeaten and (right) Lieutenant A. D. Piper, his Number One.

(*Left*) Lieutenant A. D. Piper, First-Lieutenant in H.M.S/M. Unbeaten in 1942. (*Right*) Lieutenant-Commander Teddy Woodward, Captain of H.M.S/M. Unbeaten in 1942.

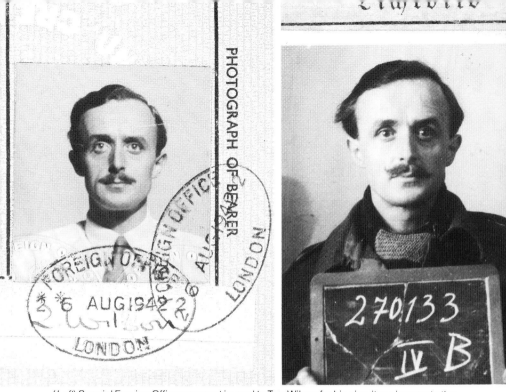

(*Left*) Special Foreign Office passport issued to Tug Wilson for his circuitous journey to the Middle-East in 1942. (*Right*) Prisoner-of-war photograph, taken on Tug Wilson's arrival in Germany in 1944, after a spell in gaol and four days in a cattle-truck.

Tug Wilson leaving Buckingham Palace, medal in hand, after receiving his DSO in July 1942.

To the previous rumours of coastal landings at Livorno to the west and Rimini to the east, there was now added another of a comforting but wildly inaccurate nature – American paratroops were reported to have been dropped in the Brenner Pass, thereby cutting off the retreat of the German army via Innsbruck to Germany. But not all the prisoners at Bologna were lulled by such wishful rumours, and among the more sceptical were Tug Wilson, Guy Greville and the newly-captured Sherard Veasey.

The camp being new and only recently filled with prisoners, no tunnels were in progress, though excavations had been rapidly begun for potential hiding-places. Nor was it easy to devise a way out over the wall and wire, which was now patrolled by German guards – though one opportunist managed to escape by clinging to the axle of a ration lorry as it left the camp unsearched. So Tug and his friends decided that the roof of a bungalow would provide the best prospect of concealment, if and when the Germans decided to move their captives elsewhere. But, alas, the camp was full of would-be escapers who were thinking along the same lines. The consequence was that they ruined each other's prospects by leaving tell-tale dirty foot-marks on the walls as they hoisted themselves up into the roofs through trap-doors to inspect various parts of the camp ceilings.

It no longer seemed feasible to use the roof, and anyway there was a considerable risk of being machine-gunned by trigger-happy guards, who would surely search the ceilings before moving off, perhaps even lobbing in the odd grenade to save themselves the trouble of climbing up and investigating. Perhaps it would be wiser to wait and hope for a chance to escape while in transit.

Meanwhile life in the camp during the next three days seemed strangely unaltered, apart from the increased tension and speculation. The rations continued to arrive and little was seen of the Germans, with all attempts to elicit information from uncommunicative sentries proving fruitless. The prisoners still didn't know what the future had in store for them. Only rumours continued to circulate – like a sort of opiate.

Then early in the afternoon of 11th September, everyone's worst fears were confirmed. The prisoners were ordered to parade with their belongings, and were lined up in rows of five. News spread that they were being moved to another camp, at Modena, which was only twenty-six miles away and, as they were being lined up, the main camp gates opened to admit a long stream of German lorries fitted with canvas hoods. The prisoners were counted into groups of thirty, with friends trying to stay together, and a lorry drew in front of each group of prisoners, who were ordered to climb into the back. Each truck just about held its complement of thirty people, standing up and packed tightly.

In the counting, Tug Wilson became detached from Guy Greville, with whom he had made plans to escape if the opportunity arose. This slip-up, though irksome at the time, was to prove by no means disastrous in its result – unlike the trick that fate played on two other officers who also became detached from their friends. A sub-lieutenant in the RNVR and a lieutenant in the Royal Sussex had teamed up together for escaping purposes, but had become detached from their friends and found themselves about to enter a truck with mainly Australians aboard. At the last moment, they were approached by two other Australians from an adjoining truck, who were anxious to join their cobbers, and a quick exchange was effected, which proved greatly to the advantage of the Aussies – as will be seen later.

With the lorries loaded, there was a delay of about a quarter of an hour while the camp was searched and a few more officers were extracted from hiding. There was plenty of shouting by the guards, but no shooting was heard. Then, without more ado, the lorries and accompanying motor-cycles revved up and drove out of the camp in a long column. Once the lorries were clear of the camp, they gathered speed and, as invariably happens in a convoy, the vehicles at the back had to belt along in order to keep up. This ruled out thoughts of jumping off and making a dash past the escorting motor-cyclists, apart from the fact that only those right at the back of each lorry had any hope of being able to jump. The others, including Tug Wilson, were packed in tightly and unable to see out.

Only when the lorries approached Modena did they slow down. Then perhaps it might have been possible to jump, but by now the city streets were lined with civilians, looking at the passing lorries in a baffled but not unfriendly way. To have jumped into their midst or dashed down a side-street, would have brought bloodshed to innocent bystanders and provided little hope of a successful escape. Anyway, as they were going to Modena Camp, it surely seemed more sensible to get there first and wait for another opportunity.

But these thoughts were short-lived. Suddenly the leading truck made a sharp turn to the left, followed by an equally violent lurch to the right, with the entire convoy doing likewise. Before the jostled prisoners had fully recovered their balance, the leading lorry shot between some high gateposts and into what was clearly not a prisoner-of-war camp, but a station goods yard. There before them, those who could see out of the cracks between the canvass covering, saw a long goods train waiting at a platform and extending far beyond, with German uniforms in every direction.

The lorries drew up, one beside each truck and the prisoners were ordered to climb down from them and get into the empty cattle-trucks that were waiting with their doors open – a lorry-load of thirty to each truck. With guards on both sides of the prisoners as they entered the trucks in a somewhat dazed state, after the recent buffeting, there was no hope of diving under a truck or making a dash for freedom. It would have been suicidal to do so. In any case there wasn't much time to think, with the guards hurrying them into the cattle-trucks to the accompanying shouts of ' *'Raus, 'Raus'* to get them out of the lorries, and '*Einsteigen*' to urge them into the cattle-trucks – the first two harsh words of German for most prisoners' ears, and destined to become all too familiar in the future.

The whole operation took only a few minutes to complete, and as the last man was safely inserted into each truck the sliding door was firmly shut. The click of the bolt on the outside sounded very final to the prisoners now hermetically sealed inside. The closing of one door was followed by the most blood-curdling screams, as one of the guards caught his finger as his comrade slammed the sliding door along. He yelled out: '*Mein Finger ist kaput!*' A voice from inside the truck added: 'So is bloody Germany!' – but, for the present, the laugh was with the Germans, apart from the owner of the crushed finger.

Tug found that there were no benches inside the cattle-truck, and not much light either, once the door was shut. However, towards one end of the far side of the truck, someone found a ventilator with an iron grid over it, about eighteen inches long and nine inches high. When this was opened, the prisoners could see better inside the truck and more air could circulate. There was a similar ventilator at the other end of the far side and it was possible for one person at a time, standing on tip-toe, to see out. Nevertheless it was somewhat claustrophobic inside the truck, and the holes were definitely too small to climb through, even if the grids could be removed. In fact the whole cattle-truck was substantially built, as some tentative probing soon revealed.

The floor of the truck was covered with clean straw and the prisoners soon organised themselves, with fifteen to either side of the truck, where they could sit or lie with their feet towards the centre and their packs down the middle, by their feet. They didn't yet know what their destination was, nor when they were likely to start. As they couldn't even see a guard from inside the cattle-truck, there was nobody to approach for information.

By now darkness was descending and there seemed nothing to do but settle down for the night and try to get some sleep. Thus began their first night in a cattle-truck and, overtaken by events and wondering where they would find themselves by the morning, they drifted off to sleep on the straw.

Next morning, as soon as it grew light, someone stood up and looked out of the ventilator. The train was not moving – and no wonder! They were still in Modena station, at the same place. They were still securely locked inside the truck, but at least they were no nearer to Germany, which was a small crumb of comfort.

About an hour later the door of Tug's truck was opened and the inmates were allowed out of the stuffy confinement to attend to the calls of nature. Looking further along the train, he could see that from several of the other trucks, too, the prisoners had been let out and were busy relieving themselves along the track, with a lack of bashfulness that many of them had learned in the desert. As one truck-load had performed, the prisoners would be ordered back inside, but in most cases the door could remain open.

The guards, though uncommunicative when it came to disclosing the destination of the train, and not disposed to smile, were by no means unreasonable at this stage. They nearly all seemed young and short of sleep. They didn't seem like hardened prison guards, but rather some second-line troops impressed into escorting prisoners in an emergency. But they were all armed and after about every fifth truck, there was a flat carriage with no super-structure, on which machine-guns were mounted and manned. Escape from the train wan't going to be easy.

Although the guards weren't going to disclose the destination of the train, the prisoners soon found out from some Italian railway workers, who in the course of their work, inspecting the wheels and the brakes, passed the word around that the train was going to Germany, via the Brenner Pass and Innsbruck, and that it would be leaving in the afternoon.

On hearing this, Tug decided that the time to leave the train was before it started, if possible. By good fortune his truck was opposite a platform and the prisoners from his truck were allowed to use a station lavatory on the platform. He had originally intended to work his way along to join his friend Guy Greville in the next cattle-truck, but before attempting to do so he went to the lavatory. In there he met an Italian workman who signalled to him to go into the closet and wait there. After a few minutes there was a tap on the window at the back and someone passed into him, through a small window at the top, a blue railway-worker's overall and a cap.

Tug lost no time in putting them on over his battledress and walked boldly out. At the door of the building the Italian workman was waiting and signalled to him to accompany him along the platform, watched with envy and admiration by his intended escaping partner in the next cattle-truck. The train hadn't yet left the station and already a prisoner had vanished.

CHAPTER 14

# Leap to Freedom

Tug Wilson was not the only prisoner to vanish from the train before it had even left Modena station. Soon another prisoner was seen leaving, under the very noses of the German guards and before the eyes of many of his incredulous fellow-travellers. Once again it was a masterly example of cool opportunism combined with quick thinking. It came about in the following way.

An Italian civilian appeared at the front of the train with a basket of fruit to sell, carried on his arm. First he did business with some of the German guards, and then got into conversation with the train-driver – a jovial figure who had already let the prisoners know that, though he was under German orders to drive his train north, his sympathies lay with his passengers. While this conversation was in progress, an idea came in a flash to an army lieutenant in one of the front trucks, from which the occupants had been let out. He had already dressed himself in some Italian-type clothing for the journey – ready for just such an opportunity as this. He quickly attached himself to the conversation and, after a few exchanges of words and gestures, he took over the basket of apples and oranges from the amenable fruit seller and started to walk nonchalantly along the train, babbling in Italian as he went and tossing an apple here and there to prisoners in the open cattle-trucks. He continued the whole length of the train until his rear view was seen heading steadily for the goods yard exit. Several weeks later he reached Switzerland.

To those prisoners who had witnessed this effrontery and opportunism, his disappearance, coupled with that of Tug Wilson, served as a spur to their determination – notably in the case of Guy Greville and Sherard Veasey and some of the travellers in their truck.

Nor was this the only spur to their determination to escape from the train. They had in their possession a useful escape weapon in the shape of an iron bar which resembled a half-sized crowbar. Sherard Veasey had come upon this handy tool as he stood with downcast

102

eyes to board the truck the previous evening. He quickly dropped his greatcoat over it on the ground and picked it up, concealed from view. It was a comforting windfall to take into the truck with him – he didn't feel quite so helpless now. In view of the well-disposed attitude of the Italian railway workers whom they met next day, who clearly preferred their recent foes, the British, to their former allies and current masters, the Germans, it seemed highly likely that the crowbar hadn't been left there by accident. At all events it was a very handy asset for Sherard Veasey, Guy Greville and the nucleus of would-be escapers, once the truck was on its way. It was out of the question to start banging away with the crowbar while the train was in the station and risk confiscation by the guards.

By mid-day more German guards arrived and were soon busy putting their kit into the tall look-out cabins built at the ends of some of the cattle-trucks, from which vantage points they could keep watch along the roofs of the trucks. Then they began closing all the sliding doors and fastening the catches, and once again the prisoners were securely locked in. By now half the day had gone, and it seemed that the train's departure couldn't be postponed much longer. There was a series of jolts, first one way then the other, followed by some whistle-blowing, before the train chugged slowly and inexorably out of Modena station. Soon it was heading northwards across the Lombardy plain.

Very soon after the train reached open country, it halted – seemingly in the middle of nowhere. The optimists on board immediately began to revive their flagging hopes. Perhaps the line ahead had been bombed by Allied aircraft? Or possibly the friendly train driver had contrived a breakdown of his engine? Maybe the Brenner Pass really had been taken by American parachutists, as previously rumoured. But just as such wishful theories were beginning to gain credence, the train started up again and continued slowly on its way. This was to be the pattern of the journey across the Lombardy Plain, punctuated by stops that raised people's hopes only to dash them again, as the train edged remorselessly on towards Germany and the heat in the trucks grew in intensity. As the sun beat down from a clear blue Italian sky, the atmosphere inside grew stifling. The prisoners stripped off much of their clothing, most of them being reduced to shorts or even underpants only. The stuffy atmosphere and lack of liquid began to sap the energy and resolve even of some of those officers who had started the journey bent on escape, but had now become dehydrated and lethargic.

Despite the heat, however, Guy Greville and Sherard Veasey and their helpers were anxious to get to work with their plan to get out of the truck with the help of the crowbar. First they had to select a spot to start. The sides of the truck were very solid, as was the floor – except for one possible weak spot where one of the floorboards was slightly worn and soft. The truck was marked on the outside: '*Hommes 40 – Chevaux 8*', and the horses' hoofs or urine could have been the cause of a small soft patch in the floor-boards. This was obviously the place to start operations with the crowbar and endeavour to bash a hole large enough to provide an exit from the cattle-truck. It had been impossible to start banging all the time the train was in Modena station, for fear of being heard by the guards and having the crowbar found and confiscated. But now was the time to get to work.

Not all the prisoners in the truck, however, were wholly in favour of these escape activities – especially as it required a certain amount of rearrangement and discomfort in an already uncomfortable situation, in order to make way for Sherard Veasey and Guy Greville and their helpers at the hole. Furthermore, some of the others were afraid of the consequences for those left in the truck, when the Germans discovered that some of their number had gone. Some of these prisoners had been as long as two, and in some cases three, years in the bag and had endured some hard times, especially in the early days. Now with the tide clearly turning against Hitler's Germany, they felt inclined to leave matters to Fate rather than ruin their long-cherished hopes of one day seeing their families again.

But such opinions were in the minority and, with the duty of captured officers to make every effort to escape uppermost in the minds of the majority, work went ahead with the hole in the floor. After some preliminary bangs with the crowbar, someone produced a primitive saw, made by cutting some teeth out of a flattened Red Cross parcel tin. It was only partly successful, but at a vital stage it enabled leverage to be achieved with the crowbar. The wooden floor proved obdurate, but gradually with much exertion and sweat a hole nearly large enough for a small man was made.

There was still the problem of how and when to squeeze through the hole, on to the track below. The position of the hole was two-thirds of the length of the truck from the front, about a foot away from the sliding door. So they should be well clear of the wheels. While they had had the chance in Modena station to look under the cattle-truck, they had checked that there was enough clearance for a prostrate body to lie safely as the rest of the train passed over it. But there remained one serious snag. One of the Italian railwaymen had told them that, in order to help the train up the gradient of the Brenner Pass once it left the flat Lombardy Plain, an extra engine would be put on at the rear end. This presented a problem, because there was a very great danger of anyone lying on the track being scooped up or hit by the apron on the front of the engine. It might be necessary for an escaper to emerge from the hole only when the train was stationary and crawl away – in which case there would be great danger of being shot by the guards, as soon as anyone crawled out from underneath the train. The only safe time to attempt a getaway would be at night. A better solution was needed, if possible.

But now, after a journey of stops and starts, in the late afternoon the train drew into a goods yard just south of Mantua – Virgil's birthplace and now known as Mantova. Here the train with the prisoners from Bologna Camp was not alone. Heart-rending cries of '*Aqua! Aqua!*' could be heard from another train of cattle-trucks alongside, packed with Italian soldiers of the famous Alpini regiment. The Germans were taking no chances with their former allies.

When the armistice was signed between Italy and the Allies, at first most Italian units fondly imagined that they would be at liberty to go home to their families (and make babies, as one Italian guard had so explicitly put it). But the Germans had other plans for them. Any unit that refused to carry on the fight was to be arrested en bloc and transported to Germany, as slave-labourers for the Third Reich, thereby serving as an example to any other Italian soldiers who mistakenly thought that their war was now over. The unfortunate Alpini were the first to be rounded up in their depot and loaded into cattle-trucks.

Now, languishing in the siding outside Mantua, they were in dire straits and their cries for water were piteous to hear – not that the prisoners from Bologna were much better off. At least it made the latter realise that they were not the only ones in distress. Then, to their surprise, and for the first time since they had left Modena, some of the truck doors were opened and one man from each truck was allowed to fetch water for his comrades in whatever containers he could muster and carry, from a tap at a signalman's cottage. In a few fortunate cases the prisoners were allowed out to relieve themselves. But still the desperate cries of '*Aqua!*' continued to reverberate across the railway-lines from the parched Italians. After an hour's delay the train with the Bologna prisoners got going and, with the cries of '*Aqua!*' growing fainter and finally dying away in the distance, Mantua itself was reached.

By the time the train left Mantua, darkness had begun to descend. This suited Guy Greville, Sherard Veasey and company, because it now seemed certain that it would be completely dark before they reached the Brenner Pass, where they hoped to make their bid for freedom.

The train moved steadily along northwards to Verona and by now Sherard Veasey and Guy Greville had hit on a possible solution to their problem of emerging from the hole in the floor without getting squashed or shot. The plan was for Guy Greville, who was a good deal smaller than Sherard Veasey, to reconnoitre through the hole and feel his way about the undercarriage of the cattle-truck and endeavour to haul himself on to the running-board and reach up to the bolt on the outside of the sliding door, so that it could be opened from the inside. Then it would be a matter of jumping out, in succession, whenever the speed of the train allowed. The plan called for great nerve and strength from Guy Greville, but he volunteered to give it a try. Now they reached Verona, and the train seemed to stop for half the night, with the result that many of the prisoners, exhausted by the heat and exertion, dropped off to sleep.

At last, around midnight, the train pulled out of the station with a jerk, and almost immediately shots began to ring out, singly and in bursts. Presumably the guards were firing at escaping prisoners – unless the shots were being fired as a deterrent. Whatever it was, the commotion served to galvanise Sherard Veasey and Guy Greville into action. Veasey, as a captured Commando, had been safe enough in Italian prisoner-of-war camps, having disposed of his green beret and only stated his name, rank and number when he had been captured. But should he reach Germany, he would be in very grave danger of being 'exterminated' if it became known that he had been captured while serving as a Commando, in accordance with the Hitler Order of 18th October 1942, concerning the handling of captured Commandos. He above all was determined to avoid being transported to Germany, if he could possibly do so. Fortunately his friend Guy Greville was equally determined.

Now was the time to put their plan into action, before it was too late. First Guy Greville groped about, with his head down through the hole, feeling for the brake shaft which was underneath the floor of the cattle-truck. Then grasping it with both hands, he pulled his body through the hole and managed to get one foot round the shaft. With the track rushing by beneath him, he managed to get the other foot on to the running-board on the outside of the cattle-truck. Hanging on for dear life, he still had the hardest part of his dangerous manoeuvre to complete. He had to reach across and grasp the running-board with one arm and then transfer his weight and grasp it with the other. Finally he had to hoist himself up to release the catch and pull the bolt of the sliding door along, so that Sherard Veasey could open it from the inside and pull his friend up to safety, back inside the cattle-truck.

It had been a nerve-racking undertaking from start to finish, and by the time Guy was safely hauled up into the truck, he was utterly exhausted. It had been an enormous strain on his arms and his nerves. It was a staggering achievement. Not only was Guy still in one piece, but now the cattle-truck door was open, and they could start jumping.

But by the time Guy Greville had been dragged aboard, the train started braking hard. They were coming to a station, which turned out to be Rovereto. There was no alternative for them but to close the sliding door and wait till the train got going again before opening it once more. They just hoped that the wait wouldn't be as long as it had been in Verona.

The minutes dragged by slowly and they could hear the guards walking up and down on the platform. At last the footsteps reached their truck. They held their breath. When the footsteps reached the door, a voice called out in German something about stupid Engländer who hadn't realised that their door was unlocked, and firmly slammed the bolt back into its original position. All Guy Greville's balancing act had been in vain.

But the prisoners inside the truck were in no mood to be denied. As soon as the train started up, they were determined to get that door open again. Luckily, with Guy Greville completely drained by his great efforts, there was an immediate volunteer to repeat the performance. His name was Peter McDowall.

Peter was a small wiry young man, with fair hair and a bristling moustache. He had bright eyes and wore a cheerful expression. Before the war he had just started as a tea-planter in Ceylon, and on the outbreak of hostilities he had immediately volunteered for military service with the Ceylon Planters Rifles. He was later commissioned into the 2nd/4th Gurkha Rifles, and it was on the 2,000 mile journey from Ceylon to Belgaum in India that he first showed a propensity for doing precarious things on moving railway trains. He was in a draft of twenty-five others, and after a break in the journey in Bangalore, the officer in charge of the draft could only count twenty-four of his men. He delayed the train's departure for ten minutes before finally giving the signal to leave. Ten minutes out of Bangalore, a head popped in at the carriage window from the blind side of the train. 'Did you miss me?' said Peter McDowall, with an impish grin. He had crept under the train at the station, and had ridden on the blind side running board until the train was well out of Bangalore.

It was the same Peter McDowall, with the same impish grin, who now volunteered to climb through the hole in the floor and reach the running-board, in order to open the cattle-truck door for his fellow officers.

Following instructions from Guy Greville, Peter crawled down through the hole, reached the running-board and stretched up for the catch. He pulled the bolt along, and in a couple of minutes he was back in the truck. For the second time they were ready to jump.

But now another problem arose. The train, which had idled its way along for much of the tedious journey, now gathered speed and belted along at an alarming rate – alarming, that is, for anyone intending to leap off. Veasey, as owner of the crowbar and a Commando by training, was to lead the way. But with the train travelling at this speed, it would be suicidal to jump.

The guards were still loosing off shots at intervals into the night, but Sherard Veasey wasn't worried so much by that. His main preoccupation was with the speed of the train and whether he dared risk jumping from it. The minutes passed by, with Sherard ready to jump, and the others waiting impatiently to follow him in their turn. Surely the train must slow down?

Eventually, after waiting for several minutes, which seemed like an eternity, the speed began to slacken slightly. Perhaps they were coming to another station, in which case it was vital to leap off before that happened, after the frustrating experience at Rovereto. The train was now passing along an embankment and going round a curve to the right. Perhaps that was why it was slowing down? It might be possible to roll down the embankment and thus get well below the arc of fire of the machine-guns. This was the place to jump all right, if only the train would slow down just a bit more.

Finally he could wait no longer. It must be now or never. He launched himself into the air, hoping to land running parallel to the train, before rolling down below the level of the wheels. He made a mighty leap, narrowly missing a telegraph pole that seemed to whiz past him. He came to earth with a crash and fell forwards before rolling roughly down the embankment. His friends inside the truck feared that he had killed himself – such had been the speed of the train and the noise that followed his leap.

In actual fact, when Sherard Veasey reached the bottom of the embankment, he realised that no bones were broken and picked himself up quickly. He had, however, wrenched his knee and gashed it quite badly – but not badly enough to prevent him from scrambling up to watch the tail end of the train disappear into the night. The best sight that he can ever recall was the red tail-light on last truck disappearing round the curve of the track and vanishing from view - without him.

Thus Sherard Veasey was on his way – eventually to Switzerland, freedom and lasting happiness, with a charming Swiss bride whom he found waiting there for him, not that either of them knew it yet.

He had led the way out of the infernal cattle-truck, and the others were poised to follow his bold lead.

# CHAPTER 15

# Dolomite Journey

Now it was Guy Greville's turn. The train was slowing down appreciably and there was no time to lose before they came to another station, in all probability.

As arranged, Guy Greville was to be number two to jump, after Sherard Veasey, whose crashing thud, as he made his bid for freedom with the train still travelling at a considerable speed, had by no means reassured those who were due to follow. Sherard Veasey had been taught in the Commandos to lessen the impact of a fall by rolling over like a parachutist landing on the ground. But there had been an almighty crash as he landed and he appeared to fall so heavily that the others had grave fears for his survival. These fears had been increased by the fact that, at the very moment at which he jumped, the carriage had flashed past a telegraph pole, and in the dark, judging from the noise, it seemed highly likely that Veasey had collided with it on his way to the ground.

Now, banishing all such unnerving thoughts from his mind, Greville was determined to make no mistake. He leapt and started running forwards in mid-air, with his legs already working like pistons, parallel with the train. The result was that he hit the ground running at considerable speed, but without falling – just as he had on countless occasions from London buses, though never at such speed nor with such urgency. Not surprisingly he found it hard to stop and, as he veered away to the left from the track, he found himself careering out of control down the embankment. He finally came to rest among some bushes at the bottom – thankfully in one piece, shaken but unharmed. The long train rattled by, and not a single shot had been fired at him.

Guy's first reaction was naturally one of great relief at landing intact and at being out of the oppressive truck and free at last. Then, having gathered himself, he clambered up the embankment and started walking back along the track, heading south in search of Sherard

110

Veasey, as previously arranged. He had only covered some five hundred yards when he came to a tunnel with what looked like barbed-wire barricades on either side.

There seemed to be no way round, as the tunnel disappeared into a high rock-face, and it soon became clear to him that it would be senseless to jeopardise his hard-won freedom by risking an encounter in the dark with a sentry very possibly guarding the tunnel. By the time he had reconnoitred, cautiously but in vain, and had finally made up his mind that his way south was barred, about half an hour had elapsed and he was still far too close to the railway-line for comfort. He felt that he had no alternative but to give up his rendezvous with Sherard Veasey and head for cover in the other direction, before the arrival of dawn and, with it, the possibility of German or Fascist Italian search parties near the railway-line. He only learned several months later that precisely the same impasse had confronted his friend Sherard Veasey as he had made his way northwards up the line as agreed, and that he too had been forced to the same inescapable conclusion and had struck off on his own towards the south-east into the mountains.

But Guy Greville wasn't without company for long. He re-traced his steps along the line, looking for cover on either side. A short distance beyond the point at which he had landed after leaping from the train he found a wood to the west, on the left-hand side at the bottom of the embankment. He quickly decided to seek cover among the trees, and as he worked his way warily into the wood he heard movement quite near him. In the moonlight he came upon his friend and recent accomplice, Peter McDowall, who had been number three to jump and had chanced upon the same wood as a desirable place for shelter. They were glad to link up and began to work their way together through the wood, which was comparatively free from undergrowth, towards its western extremity, thus removing themselves as far as possible from the railway-line.

After some ten minutes they ran into two more escapers from the same cattle-truck, who had been the next two to jump after them. The train had slowed down a lot which had made the need to jump off more urgent, before it came to a station or a halt. This had also made the alighting easier, although one of the escapers had wrenched a knee slightly – not enough to prevent him from walking, however.

The two new arrivals were a tallish Lieutenant in the Royal Artillery with fair hair and a flight lieutenant in the RAF of average size and dark-haired – both of them hitherto unknown to Guy Greville and Peter McDowall. They just happened to have been herded into the same cattle-truck at Modena. All four of them teamed up together and made for the far edge of the wood as stealthily as they could.

They peered through the fringe of trees at the westernmost edge of the wood, across an open grass field. It was now about 4 a.m. and through the darkness a few lights, presumably of houses on a slope beyond the field, could be discerned. It seemed wisest to hide where they were until dawn, which could be expected soon after 5 a.m., when they could be more sure of the lie of the land and could venture forth with caution and better visibility.

During the period of waiting a whispered discussion was held as to where they should aim for and, after a brief review of the possible courses open to them, a unanimous decision was soon reached. The courses open to them seemed to be three in number.

First, and possibly the course most in line with their duty as escaping officers, was to start heading due south until they re-joined the advancing Allied forces, which were already known to have landed on the mainland of Italy. If the wild and wishful rumours were to be believed, it might not be too long before they reached their own forces. But already some of these rumours, such as coastal landings at Rimini and Livorno or parachute drops in the Brenner Pass, had been proved false. Furthermore they were ill-equipped for a long journey of unknown duration through hostile country. They were reasonably well-shod, in army boots supplied to them in POW camp through the Red Cross, but in battledress similarly provided they would not get far before being spotted. Apart from a few bits of precious food which they had managed to stuff into their pockets before leaping from the train, and a few lire which Guy Greville had managed to hang on to from his previous escape from Sulmona, they had no other worldly goods with them to help them on their way. Guy Greville had even left his precious supply of tobacco in the truck – a disaster which he was already beginning to rue, as he felt the need to roll himself a cigarette in this period of stress. It was just as well he couldn't, as the lighting of a cigarette was known to have cost the freedom of more than one prisoner-of-war on the run. Lastly the

Escapers all. Top left: Captain Guy
Greville, MC, Royal Tanks, in
Malaya in 1945. Top right:
Lieutenant Peter McDowall, 2nd/4th
Gurkha Rifles. Bottom right:
Lieutenant Sherard Veasey, 3 and 4
Commandos.

(*Above*) Escapers' Reunion, July 1984, at the author's house in Devon. L to R: Guy Greville, Richard Broad, Desmond Haslehust and Sherard Veasey.

(*Left*) Forty-one years on. Sherard Veasey (left) and Guy Greville meet again in 1984, for the first time since their spectacular exits from a moving cattle-truck en route for Innsbruck in 1943.

fugitives had already been taken to a point so far north that a march to the south now seemed increasingly daunting.

Secondly, it might be feasible to go to ground and hide up for a few days, in the belief that the hoped-for Allied landings would still take place and that their troops might soon be within reach. In favour of this plan was the fact that it was harvest time in the vineyards and orchards of northern Italy and fruit wouldn't be hard to come by. The weather, too, was in their favour, with warm sun and clear blue skies by day and not yet too great a drop in temperature at night. But they certainly couldn't remain in hiding where they were, and this idea of hiding-up was one which might still be possible later on, if a suitable opportunity arose, but would surely lead to discovery and early re-capture if adopted now.

Their third course was to strike out to the West, up into the mountains of the western Dolomites, and go bald-headed for Switzerland, while they were still reasonably fresh and still had a little food to help them on their way. In view of the proximity of the Swiss frontier to the spot where they now found themselves, and the extreme distance from the only confirmed Allied landings on the foot of Italy, added to a certain scepticism that had by now overtaken them about the truth of the numerous rumours that had been rife in Bologna Camp and on the train, it was not hard to reach a unanimous decision to make for Switzerland. By getting there they would escape the clutches of the Germans and if, as they suspected, internment was awaiting them in Switzerland, that problem could be dealt with later. None of them wanted to fall into the hands of the Germans again and be sent to Germany.

So Switzerland it was to be – and the sooner the better. But first they must wait for the dawn, which was not long in coming. As it grew lighter they peered through the trees at the edge of the wood and were considerably taken aback when they sighted, through the half-light, a German soldier talking to an Italian farmer outside a farmhouse. The German appeared to be on his own and seemed to be asking questions. This immediately made the fugitives feel that German search parties were already out looking for escapers from the train. It wouldn't be safe to emerge from the wood at present and they looked around for somewhere safer to hide. Not far away, and still near the fringe of the wood, they came upon a deep narrow gully,

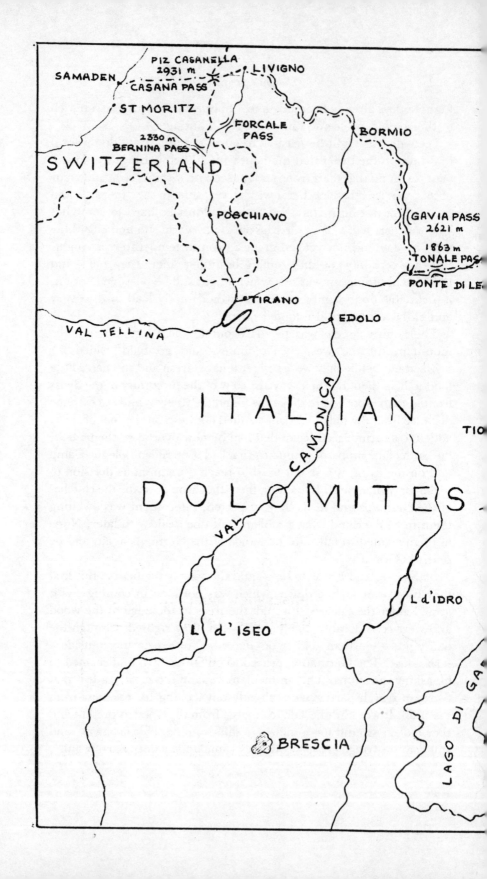

TO MERANO

TO INSBRUCK
VIA BRENNER PASS

BOLZANO

R. ADIGE

MARO

CARLO MAGNO
PASS 1682 m

R. AVISIO

MADONNA DI
CAMPIGLIO

PINZOLO

R. SARCA

TRENTO

R. BRENTA

VA

ROVERETO

HASLEHUST TRAIL ............
GREVILLE TRAIL _._._._.

SCHIO

R. ADIGE

FOSSE
LUGO

10      0      10      20      30

KILOMETRES.

VERONA

about six feet across and twice as long, between rocks, with trees growing round the rim. They quickly took cover in this gully, and went to ground.

After a while, when it had become really light, it was time for another reconnaissance and there was no longer any sign of the German who had been seen earlier. Instead, in the far corner of the field, in a sort of garden patch, there was an Italian labourer just setting about his work. He appeared to be on his own and it was decided that someone must contact him and obtain some information concerning their whereabouts and whether the coast was clear of Germans.

Guy Greville, being a captain, was the senior officer in the party, but the only one with much Italian at his command was Peter McDowall – and even he only had a smattering which he had acquired as a prisoner-of-war, largely with the aid of the camp loud-speakers which had blared forth some very patriotic and frequently inaccurate news bulletins in Italian. So Peter McDowall was sent to see if he could sound out the Italian and report back on the situation.

Peter emerged from the wood and skirted round the edge of the field until he came to the vegetable patch at the far corner. After a cautious approach he took the plunge and entered into a halting conversation with the startled Italian labourer. The man was visibly shaken and surprised. For a while he remained hesitant and suspicious. Only when Peter McDowall offered proof of his identity, in the form of a POW letter from home with his address on it, would the Italian relax and start to show a willingness to help. He told Peter that they were five kilometres south of Trento – which confirmed their suspicions of the previous night, that the train had been slowing down for a station ahead. He said that he personally couldn't do anything to help them on their way, but that he would contact a man who probably could. He also promised to bring them some food.

He seemed genuine enough, if not over burdened with intelligence, and Peter felt that he had no alternative but to trust him with the whereabouts of their hiding-place, to which he now returned to report progress to his three companions. Sure enough, about an hour later the Italian appeared with some food – bread, cheese and some apples. He told them to wait where they were until dusk, when his friend would come and guide them to safety. Meanwhile he told them that there were no Germans or Fascist Italians prowling in the vicinity. Reassured about that and satisfied with the food, they sat down to rest and doze for the rest of the day. It had been a gruelling night for all of them and from time to time they nodded off and got some welcome sleep.

By dusk they were all alert and anxious for the arrival of the man who was coming to guide them. They didn't have long after dusk to wait. An Italian duly arrived, having been told by the first one where to find them. He was a man of middle age and typical dark Italian appearance with a somewhat furtive but friendly manner. He had already been told that they wanted to make for Switzerland by the quickest route. He explained to them, with Peter McDowall acting as interpreter, that their first objective was to cross the River Adige, which ran fast down the valley from Bolzano to Trento and to the south; at the point where they were the river was to the west of the railway-line. It wasn't safe to cross it except over a bridge, because it was in spate and was very fast-moving. The nearest bridge was in the south-west outskirts of Trento, and he proposed to guide them to a man who would lead them across the Adige and set them on their way up into the hills and away from Trento. The man they were to meet was called Giuseppe Bazzanella.

The escapers emerged from their gully and followed their helper along the side of the wood and then along a track that led them through some orchards. The river was over to their left and the main road and the railway-line were to the right, both of which they avoided until after nearly an hour they came to the road. By this time they were on the southern outskirts of Trento, which is a large town stretching for a couple of miles along the Adige, from north to south. Darkness had now descended and the moon hadn't yet risen, which made it difficult to see where they were going but, more important, obscured their battledress uniform from view.

Soon the party was approaching the bridge over the river and their leader signalled to them to halt under some trees while he went ahead to find Bazzanella. He soon returned with Bazzanella and handed them over to him. Bazzanella was a thin, short, dark Italian of about thirty and also a dedicated anti-Fascist with a serious but friendly look about him. He said that the bridge wasn't guarded and that, though Trento was full of German troops, the coast was now clear for crossing the bridge. This they proceeded to do, with Bazzanella going on ahead, followed by the others in pairs fifty yards apart. The bridge was a hundred and fifty yards across and it seemed to take an awful long time to reach the other side without breaking into a suspicious run. Only two people passed them, walking in the opposite direction, gabbling loudly in Italian and taking no notice of anyone else. The River Adige was rushing by beneath them and certainly sounded turbulent.

They all heaved silent sighs of relief when they reached the other side without being challenged. Giuseppe Bazzanella wasted no time in leading them straight to his house, a distance of no more than a quarter of a mile. They were shown into a large room with chairs and couches where they were told they could rest for the night, and some hot polenta (a sort of barley-meal porridge) and ersatz coffee were provided. Their room was a big improvement on the gully in the wood, and furthermore they had crossed the Adige which meant that they had put their first major obstacle behind them on their way westwards towards the Swiss frontier.

Next morning Bazzanella appeared with some bread, coffee and a good supply of fruit – apples, plums and grapes, all of which abounded in the Trentino district, which is a noted area for fruit-growing. He told them that he was going to arrange for them to travel north-westwards into the mountains and that the first part of the journey would be covered by bus, as far as Ponte di Legno, a journey of nearly four hours. But first he must make the necessary arrangements and warn a contact of his to be ready to receive them in Bormio, beyond Ponte di Legno. It would also be necessary to provide them with some civilian clothes to wear over their battledress. It would be fatal to venture forth by day in their battledress, in which they had jumped from the train, but it would be needed for protection against the cold that they could expect to encounter in the high mountains on the Italian-Swiss border.

During the morning a motley selection of Italian clothing was produced for them to try on, and by trial and error they all managed to find some garments to hide their uniform. The result was not entirely convincing but Bazzanella felt that he could now risk leading them out to put them on a bus without attracting undue attention. He provided them with some bread and cheese and apples for the journey and at noon they set off on their way.

Bazzanella put them on the bus and paid their fares, leaving them to find their own seats, sitting in pairs several rows apart. He had previously explained that he wouldn't be accompanying them on the bus, and instructed them to get off at Ponte di Legno, from where they were to turn right and make straight for Bormio and ask for the house of his contact. They were on their own but their instructions were clear and they were glad at the prospect of putting some distance between themselves and Trento with German troops so much in evidence there by all accounts.

The bus was a smallish country-bus, about two-thirds full, with some twenty passengers. The only disconcerting event was the last-minute arrival of two Carabinieri soldiers in uniform, who took a seat at the front of the bus. Though they were in uniform, they didn't seem to be on duty in any way, and didn't even bother to look round and survey their fellow passengers. In that first week after the Italian armistice with the Allies, the military situation and the internal policing were in a state of flux, with many Italian troops regarding their war as now at an end and making by various means of travel for home, with little inclination to remain at their posts and still less of serving their erstwhile allies, the Germans. The two Carabinieri sitting in the front seat on the country-bus were in all probability on their way home. Even so it was a relief to the four disguised escapers when the two Carabinieri in uniform got out of the bus after about an hour's travelling along a road that was heading up into the mountains to the west of Trento.

The other occupants of the bus were all Italian peasants, judging from outward appearances, and the journey led them by a winding road, climbing most of the way and passing several small villages, where some of the passengers would alight and others would get on in their place. Though there was plenty of chatter among their fellow travellers, nobody attempted to engage the four escapers in conversation, nor did anyone pay much attention to them, to their considerable relief. The road took them through mainly orchard country, with a few vineyards on the south-facing slopes and jagged Dolomite peaks rising most of the way on either side, in varying shades of pink and grey with some much higher mountains looming ahead, to the west. At times the road went through solid rock, via long tunnels.

It was at a small town called Tione that the two Carabinieri got

out and the bus turned towards the north, with high mountains barring
the way ahead to the west. Now the road was climbing more steeply,
through frequent villages in scenic country, until the bus reached
another small town, Pinzolo, before climbing again to Madonna di
Campiglio and over the Carlo Magno Pass (1,682 metres) with higher
mountains close above them on the left. After a few more miles the
road reached Dimaro where it made a T-junction with a larger road,
which was the road leading from Bolzano in a south-westerly direction
to the northern extremity of Lake Como. Here the bus turned left
and after about three-quarters of an hour the road began to climb
up another pass, the Tonale (1,863 metres), from the top of which
the town of Ponte di Legno could be seen down below ahead of them.
In accordance with Giuseppe Bazzanella's instructions, this was where
the four escapers must leave the bus and make their way on foot, up
to the town of Bormio, twenty-six miles away.

On arrival in Ponte di Legno the bus deposited them in the central
square where there was quite a crowd of people milling around. The
four escapers had already spotted the road leading off to the right
in the direction of Bormio and they quickly disengaged themselves
from the throng round the bus. The last thing they wanted was to
get involved in conversation with any Italians. They were relieved
to find that there were no German uniforms to be seen and they were
soon leaving Ponte di Legno along the road to Bormio – with no
little relief that things were going according to plan so far.

It was now after five o'clock. The sun was still shining but was
beginning to sink behind the high ridges of the Dolomites in the west.
The road crossed a bridge on the outskirts of the town, over the River
Oglio, which was flowing swiftly down the valley. They walked for
another hour, following the Oglio, looking for some cover to provide
a hiding-place for the night. They were not anxious to climb too far
that evening, preferring to seek shelter down by the river, where they
could wash and drink in the fast-flowing water. They eventually found
a suitable cluster of trees nestling below the road on the left-hand side.
Before darkness fell, they freshened themselves up in the river and
ate some of the food provided by Giuseppe Bazzanella, which consisted
of some sort of solidified polenta, bread, cheese and apples. The road
had been very quiet, with only an occasional truck overtaking them
and two horse-drawn carts and three bicycles passing them from the

opposite direction without stopping. They had thought it wisest to walk in pairs about eighty yards apart for most of the way.

Although the temperature dropped considerably during the night, they all managed quite a good night's sleep under the trees, with no distractions. They ate the remains of their bread and cheese at dawn and were back on the road by the time the sun began to rise. None of them had managed to bring shaving kit with them, preferring to stuff their pockets with food and a few personal items, such as letters from home, before jumping from the cattle-truck. Now, as their beards began to sprout and their appearance grew somewhat scruffy, it was a hasty decision that they regretted. But, shaven or not, they were still free and on their way to Switzerland – with a little luck and a lot of uphill walking.

The road up to Bormio was quite an arduous climb and periodically they left the road to rest their legs, usually out of sight behind a roadside rock. On one occasion they managed to perch themselves on a promontory, from where they could look back over the route they had covered. Far below them they sighted a long column of German tanks heading south-west along the main road, from the direction of Bolzano. This finally dispelled any lingering doubts that they might have had about their decision to make for Switzerland, rather than try to make their way south. Thus encouraged, they went boldly on their way north-west to Bormio.

A long slog up to the top of the Gavia Pass (2,621 metres) led them to a mountain lake out of which the River Oglio flows. Thereafter the going was less steep, but with high mountains on their right-hand side. Finally, by late afternoon the escapers had reached the outskirts of Bormio, with only one more hill to climb up into the town, in which they had to find the contact whose name Bazzanella had given them. It had been a long day's walking, but apart from some blisters and the effects of eating some half-ripe pears, to which they had helped themselves in an orchard along the way, all four of them were in reasonable shape. All they needed now was to find their contact.

This proved to be quite a lengthy process and involved sending Peter McDowall ahead to make discreet enquiries, while the others waited by a bridge, watching the water flow by, with their backs to all passers-by. Peter approached a workman, hoping that he wasn't a Fascist, and made enquiries about the contact. The workman in turn consulted another man. In the end a third man was produced, who led the four escapers to the house of their contact. By now dusk was approaching and there was great relief when they were told by the contact that they were to spend the night in his house.

Their host was again a youngish man, probably in his early thirties, and similar in type and in his anti-Fascist outlook to Giuseppe Bazzanella, who had sent the escapers to him knowing that he was in touch with the guides who operated in the frontier mountains. He first showed them into a room at the back of his house, where they were to spend the night, and it wasn't long before they were summoned to a hot meal in the kitchen, which his wife and young daughter had prepared for them. After their arduous climb up from Ponte di Legno the warm broth was most welcome and some red vino revived their spirits. They went to bed on their fourth night of liberty feeling tired but determined to press on with their journey next day.

It had been agreed that an early start would be made, because though their Italian hosts were willing to assist the fugitives on their way, they were naturally not anxious to harbour them for any longer than necessary – knowing, as they did, the dire consequences for anyone caught doing so. These were being constantly reiterated over the radio of late, in view of the large number of recently liberated Allied prisoners-of-war who were roaming the countryside seeking shelter. Equally, the four escapers were anxious to ease the worry and end the risks involved for their kind and courageous hosts.

Their instructions were to continue up the road to Livigno, a distance of twenty-four miles, and make contact with a guide by the name of Polinelli, who lived a few miles beyond Livigno. He was a smuggler, with an intimate knowledge of the mountains to the west of Livigno, who would set them on their way over the high ridge of mountains that formed the border between Italy and Switzerland. They thanked their host and hostess and went confidently on their journey.

As the sun came out and grew stronger, they began to pour with sweat, until they were obliged to remove their battledress tunics and roll them up in a concealed bundle under their arms. In the distance they could see snow-capped mountains, and it was clear that they would be needing all available clothing before they had reached their goal. The road was even steeper, and much more winding than on the previous day, but they kept doggedly on towards their objective, with only occasional halts for food and rest. By mid-afternoon they were in sight of Livigno which was at the bottom of a particularly winding stretch of road. About four miles short of the small town, they came to a farmhouse on its own and, rather than press on into Livigno, they decided to try the farm for a drink and information about the safety or otherwise of entering the town.

To their utter amazement, in a lonely farmhouse high up in the Dolomites, they were received by two English women in their sixties, who had had Italian husbands and were now living on their own. There was no sign of their menfolk and it was assumed that they were widows, sitting out the war in a foreign land, far from the public gaze. The women were delighted to invite the four British servicemen into their farmhouse, and soon provided them with sustenance, at the same time plying them with questions about the progress of the war. For the escapers it was a relief to be able to converse in a familiar language and they soon decided to accept an invitation to sleep the night there. The farmhouse was not large, but they were shown to an outhouse at the back, well out of view from the road, where they soon made themselves comfortable.

Later they were bidden to a hot supper. It was a stew with only a few traces of meat in it, and was served with apologies for the meagre fare. But it was the best they could concoct amid the wartime shortage of meat, and it proved warm and tasty to the travellers, who devoured it gratefully. After some bread, jam and fruit, the four men were asked if they would like to listen to the BBC nine o'clock news. A very old wireless was produced from a cupboard and they all sat round and listened to their first news from home since they had been in the Egyptian Desert, more than a year ago.

Good though it was to hear voices from home, the actual news was not exactly what, in their more optimistic moments, they had hoped to hear. As far as the fighting in Italy was concerned, all the talk was of Allied bridgeheads right down in the south of the country, with no hint of landings further up the coast – and still less in the north. Little did they know that it would be another year and two-thirds before those two ladies of Livigno would be liberated, almost at the end of the war. However, the news served to stiffen their resolve to continue with all speed to Switzerland, while the going was good and before the occupying Germans spread out their dragnet to the mountains.

When they made enquiries about finding the guide, Polinelli, the two English women were most insistent that it would be unwise for the escapers to search around for him themselves, and said that they would try to get a message to him the next day. Meanwhile they would be welcome to stay where they were and rest for two nights. After covering fifty miles, much of the journey being uphill, on foot in two days, they were not averse to a day's rest in the outhouse, gathering strength for the final assault on the mountains that formed the frontier and were now looming almost directly above them to the west.

The rest day was spent mainly in sleeping, with the two English women providing hot food from time to time. They also managed to send a message to Polinelli, from whom a reply was received that he would come and collect the four escapers at 10 a.m. the following morning. Thus the fifth and sixth nights of their adventure were spent under the friendly care of two kind English women, who were far from home but still patriotic and willing to do their bit to help British servicemen on the run.

Such had been their reception that the four escapers found it tempting to linger a little longer in their comfortable and secluded billet; but all of them realised that, with freedom now within their grasp, it would be foolish to stay. The high frontier mountains to the west, despite their formidable appearance, were beckoning them on to safety. They knew they must press on and face their stiffest test.

# CHAPTER 16

# Mountain Blizzard

Polinelli duly arrived to guide them. He turned out to be a tough-looking character in his thirties, with an outdoor mountaineer's complexion. He was of medium build and wiry physique. He seemed confident that the coast was clear in Livigno, as far as Germans or Fascist Italian police were concerned. Nevertheless, as a precaution and to attract less attention, he made them split into two parties as he guided them to his house on the far side of Livigno. Of the Italians whom they had met, Polinelli was by far the most communicative. He was almost garrulous.

He said he was going to take them up through the tree belt to a hut at the base of the climb up to the Casana Pass, up which lay the route by foot into Switzerland, with Piz Casanella (2,931 metres) just beyond the frontier to their right. There was no frontier wire to be negotiated – the mountain ridge itself forming a natural and forbidding barrier. He would guide them to a hut, where he would spend the night with them before starting them off on their final ascent the following day and pointing out their way to Switzerland – and to freedom.

Livigno, nowadays a flourishing ski-resort and a strangely situated mecca for searchers after duty-free goods, lies along a wide valley, with the mountains that form the frontier with Switzerland rising on the western side. As one faces the mountains, there is a mountain road to the left which leads up and along the Forcale Pass (2,330 m), over to the top of the Bernina Pass in Switzerland. There is a frontier post near the top, but it was out of the question for the escapers to take this somewhat easier route through the mountains and risk capture at the frontier post. They had to take the unguarded footsloggers' and smugglers' route up the Casana Pass in front of them. The going would be much tougher, but their prospects of success would be infinitely increased by taking this route.

They walked through the trees and on to the open mountain with Polinelli until he led them to the hut, nestling below a long steep ascent.

They ate some bread and cheese which had been provided for their journey by the two English women, and on a stove in the hut Polinelli brewed up some ersatz coffee, using wood that had been left in the hut by previous occupants. The stove provided heat for most of the night.

Polinelli set them on their way the next morning, indicating volubly the route that they must take up to the top of the Casana Pass high above them. They thanked him and went forth full of determination to accomplish the final challenge of their journey.

All went well at first, but after about two hours the sky began to cloud over, for the first time since their journey through the Dolomites had begun. But they pressed on undaunted. After some four hours the clouds had descended and were looking ominous. Visibility grew rapidly less, but still they pressed hopefully on towards the ridge at the top. Finally, after five hours of increasingly difficult climbing, they found themselves well and truly enveloped in a blizzard, with visibility ahead of them reduced to virtually nil. It would have been hopeless to continue.

All they could do was to try to retrace their footsteps and return to the refuge of their hut. Even this proved impossible, because, in order to make sure that they didn't get lost on the mountain, they had to follow a stream down to the road that led south from Livigno, and in so doing they missed the hut.

However, they were safely off the mountain and on the road. They made their way back in search of Polinelli at his house, but when they got there he was nowhere to be found. Just when they were wondering what on earth to do, they met an Italian who said that he might be able to find them another guide. Soon a second guide arrived and stated that he was prepared to take them up the mountain the following day, when the storm was over, and put them on the right route to the frontier. He would select a route to the left of where they had made their unsuccessful attempt.

The second guide was of slighter build than Polinelli, and taciturn by comparison. Furthermore, whereas Polinelli had been prepared to provide his services to them for nothing, this second guide wanted payment for the services that he was about to render. Guy Greville produced his small amount of Lire and offered it as payment. But the guide demanded more. He pointed to Guy's army boots and indicated that he wanted them in payment, offering in exchange his own civilian shoes. Guy Greville, at five feet eight, was the shortest member of the party, and he also wore the smallest shoes – the only pair that would fit the guide. Feeling that he was in no position to refuse this uneven exchange, he grudgingly assented with considerable misgiving – a move that was to cause him much agony in the near future. But at least it had secured for them the services of a guide, with which they certainly couldn't dispense, if they were to reach their goal at the second attempt.

The guide also asked for a chit addressed to the British authorities, stating what services he had rendered to escaping British servicemen. This was soon provided and the party moved off behind their new guide to spend the eighth night of their journey sheltering in the trees at the foot of the mountain. They sincerely hoped that it would be the last before reaching freedom. Their morale had received a dent from their first abortive attempt, but they were still determined to summon up enough energy and courage to succeed.

After a cold and uncomfortable night, in which little sleep was achieved, the guide led them off as soon as it was light and took them up through the trees to the open mountain. Up above them they could see the snow line and what they thought was the crest of the mountain range. The guide pointed out the route up to the top of the Casana Pass and told them that after four or five hours' climbing they would be over the border and into Switzerland. He had wished them luck and left them to make their own way.

The climb proved steep and arduous, but they made steady progress for the first two hours. Not surprisingly Guy Greville's pointed Italian shoes began to hurt, pinching his toes and causing bad blisters on both heels. But he was determined not to lag behind and he forced himself to keep going.

As they got higher and reached the snow-covered part of the mountain, Peter McDowall experienced difficulty with his breathing and became increasingly distressed – so much so that the others offered to carry him. But Peter would have none of this and battled on with great determination.

Several times they thought they were reaching the crest of the ridge, only to find that there was a further ridge in front of them. At last they reckoned that they really had come to the top, after five hours of hard slog, and could look down to the other side, which they sincerely hoped was Switzerland. At this point they heard shouting further down the mountain behind them and, on looking round, they sighted a man on his own joining their tracks at a tangent and yelling to them. He was in civilian clothes and wanted them to wait for him. But at this stage they were in no mood to take chances and hang around. Their immediate preoccupation was to press on and make sure that they really were well inside Switzerland. So they continued, with the man still following and shouting to them intermittently.

By now the going was much easier and mostly downhill. Guy Greville's feet were still hurting him and his heels were getting rubbed very sore indeed. But nothing was going to deter him now. Likewise, Peter McDowall was able to keep going, and as they lost height so his breathing eased. They kept on and on, and rather to their surprise they met nobody. After continuing for at least another four hours they all felt that they really must be well inside Switzerland by now, and sure enough they soon spotted quite a large body of men in uniform marching along a road below. As they approached, it became clear that they were Swiss troops out on border patrol.

The Swiss soldiers welcomed the four weary fugitives with open arms and confirmed that they were safely in Switzerland and that they would take them to the village of Samaden for food and rest, before being sent on to a reception camp at Wil, to the east of Zürich. Though Samaden, which is a few miles north-east of St Moritz, is in the Italian-speaking part of Switzerland, the soldiers spoke either Swiss-German or French. So Guy Greville, who spoke French, took over the interpreting from Peter McDowall, who had previously handled the Italian.

On arrival in the village of Samaden at what appeared to be a military headquarters, from which the platoon of soldiers that the escapers had met had been sent out on a routine patrol, late afternoon tea was provided with bread, butter and jam. The travellers were relieved to be able to rest their weary limbs and to tend their sore and bleeding feet. Guy Greville's heels were in a ghastly mess, with not only the skin but also much of the flesh rubbed off, almost down to the tendons at the back. They took a week to recover.

It was explained to them that their status was that of *évadés*. Under the Geneva Convention, dealing with the treatment of prisoners-of-

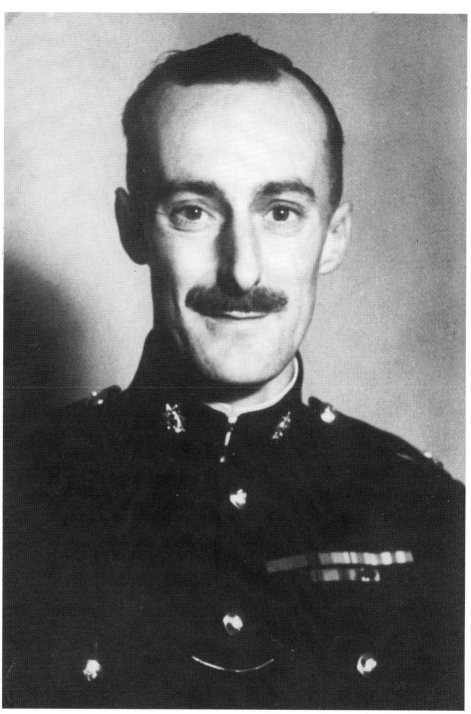

Major Desmond Haslehust, The Worcestershire Regiment, after the war and before taking Holy Orders.

Seven days before he was shot, Pope John Paul shaking hands in Rome with The Very Reverend Canon Haslehust, to mark the latter's Silver Jubilee as a priest.

war, it was laid down that ex-prisoners-of-war who escaped and crossed the frontier into a neutral country were to be given sanctuary and sustenance, and not to be imprisoned. They were free to move around within the country of refuge, though, on strict orders from the British Legation in Berne, they could not cross the frontier and depart. They were not to be interned, but, with the increasing number of escapers arriving from Germany and, particularly recently, from Italy, it was agreed by the British and Swiss authorities that the *évadés* would be quartered together in suitable areas and administered by their own officers.

It was a relief to the new arrivals that they were to be granted this relatively free status of *évadés*, and were not to be put behind barbed wire again as internees, as they had feared.

The attitude of the Swiss was very different towards the man who had been shouting on the moutain and had now caught up with the others. He turned out to be an Italian doctor who, for some reason, needed to get out of Italy. Despite his indignant protestations, he was finally told that he was regarded as an illegal entrant from a neighbouring country, and therefore to be interned, and not to be treated as an escaped prisoner-of-war – and thus not eligible for the status of *évadé*. No amount of renewed shouting would alter this umpalatable verdict – nor did he endear himself to the Swiss, or alter this decision, by his continued protests.

After a short rest and clean-up, the four *évadés* were given a substantial meal of meat stew and vegetables, accompanied by some warming schnapps. After all their hard slog in the Dolomites, they spent the ninth night since they had jumped from the train near Trento in reasonably comfortable army bunks at Samaden – happy and thankful that their troubles and exertions were now at an end. They were glad, too, that they had made their dash for Switzerland while the going was good and before winter had set in. One experience of a mountain blizzard had proved quite enough.

\*

With Guy Greville and his companions safely in Switzerland, it is now time to return to Modena station and follow the vicissitudes awaiting his former partner in escape, Tug Wilson, after he had managed to leave the train before it had even started on its eventful journey through the Brenner Pass to Germany with its load of Allied prisoners-of-war. But before returning to Tug Wilson, one further digression remains to be explored – the escape from the same Innsbruck train carried out by Captain Desmond Haslehust, whose path is destined to cross that of Tug Wilson later on, via some very different and far-reaching experiences at large in Italy.

CHAPTER 17

# 'Are you English?'

Captain Desmond Haslehust, of the Worcestershire Regiment, a tall
slim regular soldier, was another victim of the events which had
overtaken Tug Wilson, Guy Greville and a thousand others at Bologna
on the fateful morning of 9th September 1943, and had resulted in
their reluctant presence aboard the train to Innsbruck, from Modena
station. Desmond Haslehust was as determined as they were to avoid
deportation to Germany. The method of escape which he contrived,
as well as the outcome of his adventures, were both of them a variation
on the escaping theme that seems to justify a short digression in Tug
Wilson's story. Like Guy Greville, Desmond Haslehust chose the same
starting-point for his bid for freedom – a hole in the cattle-truck floor.
But thereafter his movements make an interesting comparison, and
his path later converges with that of Tug Wilson.

In September 1943 Desmond Haslehust was twenty-five and, after
several campaigns on active service, had reached the rank of captain and
the frustrating status of prisoner-of-war. Born in Plymouth, he had been
educated at Malvern College and trained as a regular infantry officer
at Sandhurst. Soon after being commissioned in the Worcestershire
Regiment he was posted in early 1938 with the 1st Battalion to Palestine.
On the outbreak of World War II his battalion was moved to the Sudan
as a counter to the threat of Mussolini's army in Eritrea, and in
Abyssinia, which Italy had added to her colonial empire. When Italy
entered the war on 10th June 1940, the Worcestershires played a major
part in the fighting in Eritrea, which was far more bloody and arduous
for those who actually took part, than for those who merely read the
newspapers in England and reckoned the Italians to be traditionally a
pushover. Those who fought the battle for Keren, including Desmond
Haslehust, could testify otherwise.

When Addis Ababa fell on 3rd April 1941 to British and Empire
troops (the latter including in those days South African and Rhodesian
volunteers), the way became clear for units to be moved to the Western

Desert to oppose Rommel and his Afrika Korps, and the 1st
Worcestershires were among those transferred.

By this time Desmond Haslehust had been promoted to the rank
of captain and was soon actively engaged in penetrating forays into
enemy-held territory with formations known as 'Jock columns', which
were devised as a counter to Rommel's own incisive thrusts. Jock
columns were originally led by Brigadier Jock Campbell, later killed
in action, and consisted of armoured cars with twenty-five pounder
guns, accompanied by lorried infantry. For his participation in this
phase of Desert warfare, Desmond added a second Mention in
Despatches to his first, which he had earned in the campaign in Eritrea.
But then his luck ran out. He happened to be in the wrong place at
the wrong time. The place was Tobruk and the time was 7 a.m. on
21st June 1942, when the important harbour fell into the hands of
Rommel's Afrika Korps – and with it many thousands of prisoners.

Thus it was that in September 1943, after fifteen months in the
bag, Desmond Haslehust found himself locked in a cattle-truck at
Modena, on board a train that was transporting Tug Wilson, Guy
Greville and nearly all the other prisoners-of-war from Bologna Camp
to a further spell of captivity. Although Bologna wasn't a 'bad boys''
camp, it was nevertheless for being a 'bad boy' that Desmond
Haslehust had been sent there. When a batch of prisoners-of-war was
required to be sent to Bologna in early August 1943 from Chieti Camp,
the commandant of the latter took the opportunity of including in
the draft all the members of the escape committee, whose names had
been supplied to him by one of his camp stooges, together with others
who had made a nuisance of themselves and incurred his displeasure.
Desmond Haslehust had qualified for inclusion by making disparaging
statements about his gaolers in his letters home, all of which had to
be censored by the Italians before despatch via the Red Cross in
Geneva. This misdemeanour had earned him four weeks in the
'cooler'. He was also rightly suspected of tunnelling.

Once inside the truck at Modena, just as Guy Greville and Sherard
Veasey had found a certain amount of opposition to their proposal
to make a hole in the floor through which to escape, so in his truck
Desmond Haslehust encountered the same antipathy from some of
the more resigned prisoners, who preferred to endure their fate rather
than rock the boat and invite reprisals from the Germans.

However, there were half a dozen officers who were prepared to work hard on a scheme to remove some floorboards. By converting two table-knives smuggled from Bologna into rudimentary saws, by rubbing the blades together at right-angles in order to form small teeth, they set to work in relays. Before they could insert their improvised saws into the floorboards, they first had to pare off slivers of wood from the floor by using a safety razor-blade. It proved a slow and sweaty job in an already over-heated atmosphere, but they stuck doggedly at it, as the train travelled across the sunbaked Lombardy Plain. Once they were through one of the planks, which ran transversely across the truck, it was possible to lever the plank up from the floor, just sufficiently to be able to pull the end of it from its slot in the iron girder that ran along the side of the cattle-truck. With three planks thus removed there was a hole sufficiently wide to allow a person to sit on the floor and dangle his legs down through the hole, at the same time holding on to the plank in front of him.

When the train reached Mantua in the late afternoon and came to a halt next to a train-load of parched Italian soldiers who were wailing plaintively for water, a few of the trucks containing the Bologna prisoners were opened briefly to enable the occupants to relieve themselves. Desmond Haslehust seized this unexpected opportunity to hide behind a pile of railway sleepers near the line. His fellow inmates were ordered back into the truck and the door was once again firmly locked by the guards. Desmond's colleagues reckoned that he might be getting away with his spur-of-the-moment escape, when one of them saw him through the grill over the ventilator being rudely escorted back to the truck at the point of a bayonet, threateningly wielded by a blond young German soldier who had found him crouching behind the pile of sleepers. Desmond had only just succeeded in calming the angry youth by gesturing that he had merely been relieving himself and was too bashful to do it in public view. So he was returned to the cattle-truck – back to square one, but still narrowly unscathed. This abortive bid for freedom had served to whet his appetite for more.

When the train eventually left Mantua, darkness was not far away, and darkness was what the would-be escapers were waiting for. They realised that in dropping through the hole on to the track, and letting the train pass over their prostrate bodies, they would be running a considerable risk of being hit by any undercarriage there might be on the trucks behind them. But as far as they had been able to see on their last brief glimpse from outside the truck at Mantua, no auxiliary engine had yet been coupled to the rear of the train.

Six of them, all desperate to avoid further years of captivity in Germany, elected to use the exit via the hole in the floor which had been completed with so much sweat and toil. Lots were drawn to decide the order in which they would descend through the hole, and the idea was that, as soon as it was dark enough, the first man would leave the truck immediately after the next halt in open country. Obviously to do so while the train was in a station, and thus be left lying on the track in full public view, would be courting disaster. Equally, it would only be safe to take the plunge while the train was still going slowly, just after re-starting and before it had gathered speed.

Fortunately this particular train had seemed prone to inexplicable halts in the middle of nowhere in particular and, sure enough, as darkness was descending, a few miles south of Verona, as it turned out, just such a halt occurred. The escapers grabbed the few belongings that they could take, which wasn't much because they needed both hands free for hanging on as they let themselves down through the hole. Prisoners-of-war who had known what it was to be destitute of all possessions were notoriously reluctant to be parted from the few belongings that they had managed to acquire. But now only small items that they could stuff inside their shirts or into their trouser pockets could be taken with them. The rest would have to be left behind.

As the train lurched into motion, the first escaper sat ready to lower himself down through the hole, mindful of the fact that the quicker he could be gone the easier it would be for those hoping to follow, before the train gathered too much speed. Number one descended on to the track without a hitch and number two lost no time in following him. By the time number three descended, the train was beginning to go uncomfortably fast; but he just made good his exit. The first 'stick' of three escapers had dropped successfully through the hole. It could only be hoped that they had all landed safely and hadn't been hit as they lay on the track by anything projecting under the train. At least there had been no shots fired, so with luck they might have got clean away.

Now the train reached Verona. There was a very long delay and it was feared that they might be waiting for an extra engine to be attached at the back. However, there was no ominous shunting or jolting to indicate this – merely an exceedingly tedious hold-up without moving. Some of the prisoners fell asleep.

At last the train slowly began to creak into motion and the next batch of escapers prepared to make their bid for freedom, considerably heartened by the apparent success of the first batch. Desmond Haslehust was to be the third to drop and knew that he would have to grab his chance without delay. Again the first two dropped as quickly as they could, as soon as the train was clear of Verona station.

Desmond Haslehust, at six feet tall, wasn't really built for acrobatics, but he was lean and determined, with no time to linger. He sat down on the floor of the cattle-truck and let his legs dangle down the hole, relieved to find how high the clearance was above the track. Then he held on to the floorboard in front of him with both hands, and let his feet down to the track. For a few strides he more or less ran along between the rails before letting go with his hands and falling forwards on to the ground. Several cattle-trucks rattled past above him without touching him, as he lay there with his arms outstretched in front of him, scared stiff and motionless.

His ordeal was soon over. He had planned to continue lying there, rather than get up too soon and thus offer a silhouetted target to any machine-gunners who might be on the alert, when the train had passed over him. But as it drew away from him into the darkness, he permitted himself a quick upward glance at the rear light on the end of the last truck.

His brief elation at this gratifying sight was rudely interrupted by sudden bursts of shots coming from the train and rending the night air. In his vulnerable position he felt sure that the shots were being aimed down the track towards him. This was no place to hang around and, crouching low, he made a quick dash down the right-hand embankment, straight into some very prickly brambles. He could feel blood trickling on his face and hands, but the important thing was that he had succeeded in making his exit from the truck without damage to his long limbs. He decided to remove himself from the scene of his escape without delay. He set off into the night to seek a hiding-place before daylight. It was now 1 a.m.

Desmond was wearing khaki-drill trousers and a khaki shirt, both

of which had been dyed blue with a mixture of ink and wine, in order
to give him a somewhat civilian appearance. His brown army officer's
boots he had cut down and converted into shoes. Into his pocket he
had stuffed an army emergency ration in a flat tin, a very small Italian
pocket-dictionary and a handkerchief. As befits a British infantryman,
he had also taken with him a safety razor and a packet of blades,
received in a next-of-kin parcel sent from home. On his wrist he wore
the gold wristwatch which had accompanied him through three years
of campaigning with his regiment, and had somewhat surprisingly
survived the many POW camp searches and remained in his
possession.

After staggering gropingly through some vineyards, in pitch
darkness, and several times nearly beheading himself in collisions with
the support wires holding up the vines, he came to a road. He decided
to cross it, in order to put more distance between himself and the
railway-line.

As he did so, a figure stood up out of the ditch on the far side of
the road. As far as Desmond could see in the dark, it was a man
wearing battledress. Desmond approached him and on the spur of
the moment said: 'Are you English?' 'I'm Scottish,' was the reply
– enunciated with sufficient native accent to back up this proud
assertion.

The Scottish figure in the dark was Lieutenant John Lewis
Cameron, of the Cameron Highlanders, who had also managed to
bale out of the train – not through a hole in the floor, but through
a door which had been forced open in another truck. He had been
walking cautiously along the road and had taken refuge in the ditch
on hearing Desmond Haslehust approach.

Even though John Cameron wasn't going to admit to being English,
he was only too glad to throw in his lot with a member of an allied
nation, being gregarious by nature. Though the two of them had been
in the same camp at Bologna, they hadn't previously met. But they
immediately teamed up and set off together to find shelter before dawn.

Their position was somewhere to the north of Verona, not far out
of the city. After stumbling in the dark through more vineyards,
avoiding decapitation by the supporting wires, they eventually reached
a humble farmhouse. With little hesitation they decided to take pot
luck and ask for shelter. They knocked on the door and, not

surprisingly at that ungodly hour, the farmer and his wife in the background stood aghast, quivering with fear. Using what little Italian he had at his command, backed up by some School Certificate Latin which seemed to help, Desmond Haslehust explained who he and John Cameron were and that they wanted shelter. The farmer's fear, understandable in any case, was heightened by the fact that his farmhouse was a mere five hundred yards from a German anti-aircraft unit. However, he agreed to allow the two fugitives to spend the rest of the night in his air-raid shelter at the back of the house. But first his wife insisted on fetching a bowl of water and cleaning up the blood which had now become extensive on Desmond's face, forehead and hands. Should the two officers be discovered in hiding, they were going to make out that they had put themselves into the shelter unbeknown to the farmer.

When daylight came they were summoned into the house and given some bread, fruit and acorn coffee for breakfast. Then some more suitable clothes were produced and Desmond had a much-needed wash. He found that the sweat from his exertions in the truck and from his subsequent scrambling across country had caused the home-made dye in his clothes to run all over his body. When he took his shirt off, his body looked as if it had been painted with woad. John Cameron was far too conspicuous in his battledress, supplied to prisoners-of-war by the Red Cross when the garments in which they had been captured wore out – in many cases they were captured in just a shirt and a pair of khaki shorts, worn for fighting in the heat of the Libyan desert, but inadequate for a winter in Europe. The farmer produced an Italian workman's jacket for each of them, and a pair of plus-fours for John Cameron. With no stockings to go with the plus-fours, the resulting appearance was distinctly odd, with an expanse of leg showing between the end of his trousers and his ankle socks in his black army boots. Cameron hoped that he would pass for some sort of Italian mountaineer.

John Cameron was a young medical student from Kingussie, near Aviemore, and had interrupted his studies in the early stages in order to enlist on the outbreak of war. He was a couple of years younger than Desmond Haslehust and had also been captured in the Desert fighting. He was of medium height and average build. He was clean-shaven with black hair and a sallow complexion, which helped towards

his disguise as an Italian. He was of cheerful disposition and talked
with a moderate Scottish accent, which permeated the small amount
of Italian that he managed to utter.

The two fugitives wanted to get up into the foothills of the Dolomites
which they could see rising quite steeply in the distance – their
immediate surroundings near Verona being flat and too inhabited
for safety. Between the farmhouse and the hills lay the River Adige,
which flows swiftly down from Trento, through Verona, on its way
to the Adriatic coast. The Adige had to be crossed and to attempt
to do so over a bridge in Verona would be inviting arrest. To try
to swim across it would be too dangerous, they were told, and the
plan was for one of the farmer's many relations to procure a boat
and row them across.

Late in the afternoon a youth appeared with the news that he had
borrowed a boat and was ready to put them across the Adige. They
thanked their hosts and walked across some fields and through some
orchards to the bank of the river. They soon realised why it was
considered too dangerous to swim across, when they saw the water
rushing past at great speed.

The boat was a small blunt-sterned dinghy, of the kind used by
yachtsmen for rowing themselves ashore from a mooring to the bank.
It looked adequate for its present purpose. They stowed themselves
carefully aboard and the youth struck out with his oars towards mid-
stream. Though he struggled manfully to reach the far bank, it soon
became obvious that they weren't going to land at a point anything
like immediately opposite their starting-point. The fierce current
carried them far down stream and to their horror they realised that
willy-nilly they were going to land well within the built-up outskirts
of Verona. Houses began to appear on the bank as they were swept
by. But the youth at the oars remained calm and determined and
gradually they emerged from the main stream, into calmer water,
and were able to edge towards the bank. After about twenty minutes
of hard rowing and uncontrolled drifting, they were thankful to get
ashore.

It was late afternoon and they were right in Verona. They were
by no means confident in their civilian disguise, but there was no
option but to head northwards without delay, in an attempt to get
out of town. They hadn't gone far before they came to a company of

German infantry resting by the side of the road. Haslehust and Cameron just kept walking steadily on – there was no point in turning back or running away. The Germans fortunately were busy chatting together among themselves and took no notice of the two scruffily disguised escapers, whose morale received an encouraging boost and no small relief at this first encounter with the enemy.

By now they had reached what appeared to be a slum area of Verona and, rather than be caught on the streets after the 8 p.m. curfew of which they had been warned, they decided to seek shelter in a very humble dwelling which had a stable on the ground floor, with living quarters above. Once again the family of peasants appeared to be scared stiff but were friendly. The two escapers were allowed shelter in the stable and were later provided with some food, on condition that they would be gone early the next morning. This suited them well, as it was their intention to get up into the hills and mountains to the north of Verona as soon as possible and then take stock of their situation there.

They set off in the morning and headed for a village on the way to the mountains called Montecchio. They came to the Casa Canonica, the residence of the local parish priest. He, like the peasants, was anxious to help but was very apprehensive. He pointed out that the Germans were liable to call at his house at any time, and that the local Fascists, who were now re-emerging and getting their arrogance back, were in the village. It was out of the question for him to harbour British officers on the run, but he would lead them to someone else who might well hide them for the present. They were guided to the humble abode of a man who was rabidly anti-German and anti-Fascist, though he wasn't at that time an active member of the Partisans. He agreed to put them up for the present, and thus it was that Haslehust and Cameron found themselves having to sleep three in the only bed available.

Fortunately they weren't there long, as the next day two young men, who had been in the Italian Air Force and had taken to the hills since the armistice, rather than be impressed into service with the German Luftwaffe, came and collected the two British officers and led them further up into the hills to what they called a *malga*. This was a mountain hut, used by farmers when they move up in the summer to reach the high grazing pastures for their cattle and goats.

In this secluded hide-out, Haslehust and Cameron spent the next two weeks, safe from detection but waiting impatiently for news of any signs of the approach of Allied troops. The two Italians, who were in civilian clothes, made periodical journeys on foot down to the village to get bread and the bare necessities to keep the four of them fed. It soon transpired that food wasn't all that these two young airmen were after, for they were exceedingly randy and, after every excursion to the village for provisions, they would return and boast of their conquests and sexual prowess. Anything that appeared puzzling to the limited vocabulary of their audience was readily elucidated by means of unmistakable gestures and mime. The airmen also made contact with the Partisans, with a view to passing on the British officers into their care. The latter unfortunately remained very much in the dark concerning the fighting in the south of Italy, but, like most escaped prisoners-of-war at that time, they remained optimistic about the prospect of Allied forces arriving in their direction. For this reason they ruled out all idea of heading for Switzerland, fearing that such a course, apart from being by no means easy across the mountains, would only lead them to a blind end, culminating in further internment. Their duty, they felt was to endeavour to join their own forces as soon as it was practical to do so. But until they could get some encouraging and concrete news, to replace the abundant supply of wild rumours, they would be well advised to remain up in the mountains in comparative safety.

Finally, contact was made on their behalf with a group of active Partisans, the leader of whom, Luciano Dal Cero, came to fetch them. He was a very brave and honoured man, of whom more will be heard in the epilogue of this book. They set off early one morning, after two weeks living in the *malga*, and climbed for hours, right up into the Dolomites. After passing through a village with a church, called Fosse, to their surprise and relief they reached a hotel nestling under a very high mountain, known as the Sega di Ala. This was where they were to stay.

It was a small hotel, with eight bedrooms, occupied by Luciano Dal Cero and his aunt, plus a few friends. There were no outsiders in residence and soon Haslehust and Cameron were welcomed into the community and, for security's sake, were given Italian names. Desmond Haslehust became Paulo, and John Cameron was Attilio, which were the names of Luciano's two brothers, who were elsewhere at this time.

Here they spent a month, biding their time in reasonable comfort and safety. One alarming incident caused a flutter, when some Germans in a lorry turned up unexpectedly outside the front door. While Paulo and Attilio made themselves scarce, two small sons of one of the guests began chatting to the German soldiers. Their mother was terrified that they might let drop a remark that would lead the Germans to suspect the presence in the hotel of two British officers. However, even at their tender age, the two boys had enough security sense to keep quiet – one of them Franco Galdiolo, being destined to become a major-general in the post-war Italian army, and the other, Fabbio, a successful businessman in Pisa.

The surrounding country was magnificent. Some of the time was spent in reconnoitering the area for possible dropping zones for Allied weapons and supplies for the Partisans, if this could be arranged. Haslehust and Cameron were also able to send a message via a Partisan who was going to Rome, for delivery to the British Minister in the Vatican, reporting that they were still alive and safe. The upshot of this message was that Desmond's father was told by the War Office that his son had reached Switzerland and, through some relations in Lausanne, enquiries were made which, hardly surprisingly, proved abortive.

Unlike Guy Greville and his companions, who were more sceptical about the possibility of the arrival of Allied troops in the area of northern Italy and had gone bald-headed from the start for the Swiss frontier, Haslehust and Cameron, after successfully avoiding recapture, were finding it hard to make a move towards the still distant Allied lines. Furthermore they were up against the inescapable fact that, after the early days of chaos in Italy immediately following the armistice, the military and police situation had now stabilised. Whereas it had for a time been possible to travel south by train without identity papers, this possibility was getting increasingly remote, owing to the re-emergence of the Fascist police and the tightening-up of controls for all travellers. It seemed that, though still at large, they had missed the bus.

They had long discussions between themselves and with their Partisan friends as to where they should go. They felt that they couldn't impose upon their generous hosts indefinitely; nor did they wish to endanger them further. After a month at the hotel, Desmond Haslehust decided that some positive action was required, and he set off alone to the village of Fosse, through which they had passed previously.

In Fosse, which nestles beneath the high Corno d'Aquiglio, on which many gun emplacements sited by the Austrian army during World War I were still visible, he called at the house of the parish priest, Don Domenico Veronesi, himself a former army chaplain in the First World War. He was a charming grey-haired man in his late fifties, of short and sturdy stature, and he welcomed Desmond to his two-storey presbytery, where he lived with three of his brother's children for company. The eldest of these, a girl named Imelda, was twenty and she ran the household, cooking not only for Don Domenico but also for her early teen-aged brother and sister. Don Domenico was an educated but down-to-earth man, with a ready sense of humour. He was also a deeply spiritual man, whose example was to exert a great influence on the young army captain who was now his guest.

After a week's separation, during which John Cameron felt increasingly lonely, with only Italians to talk to and a still very limited vocabulary at his disposal, he too moved down to the presbytery. Desmond had made good use of his pocket dictionary and each night he systematically looked up and learned new words. With luck he remembered half of them the next morning, and in this way he gradually enlarged his vocabulary. A limiting factor was the small range of topics among the people he met – the conversation being confined mainly to crops, cows and everyday necessities and the news and rumours of the war, with the peasants' use of dialect adding to the difficulty. It wasn't until the unification of Italy, under Garibaldi, that there was one Italian language, based on that spoken in Florence. Even now a Piedmontese can barely understand a Neapolitan's dialect – the variations being more extreme, and involving a greater number of differing words, than is the case when, say, a Yorkshireman is turned loose among rural Devonians, or vice versa. Even educated families throughout Italy sometimes speak dialect at home and official Italian elsewhere. This was an extra difficulty for escaped POWs to overcome. Still, some reasonable progress was achieved and this resulted later in Haslehust's being taken for a southern Italian by a priest in the confessional who couldn't see him through the grill. He felt he had at least got somewhere!

The focal point of the presbytery was the kitchen, where there was a sort of witches' cauldron suspended on chains over an open hearth. Desmond Haslehust felt that he ought to offer to help with the kitchen chores, but, in Italy in 1943 at any rate, the idea of a male raising a finger to help in what was regarded as women's work, was utterly prosposterous to Italian peasant womenfolk. On one occasion Desmond prevailed on Imelda to allow him to make some butter, from milk from the house cow. For almost an hour he shook a container resembling a chianti bottle, until his arms were aching. Finally, with no little pride of performance, he managed to produce a sizable lump of butter and gleefully presented it to Imelda. He was looking forward to sampling his share of the fruits of his labours, but to his mortification Imelda took one look at it and without more ado consigned it to the pasta which was simmering away in the cauldron. This action, though doubtless enriching the pasta, had the effect of dampening Desmond's ardour for housework. He didn't volunteer again!

Here once again Haslehust and Cameron began to feel that they were endangering the whole household by their continued presence, yet their plans to make a move southwards with the aid of the Partisans were still failing to materialise. To ease the situation at Don Domenico Veronesi's, it was arranged for them to move to the nearby village of Lugo, to stay with Don Domenico's brother Beniamino and his younger children. After nearly a month spent in the enjoyable company of Don Domenico, it was quite a wrench to bid farewell, but they felt that they had to make a move, because it seemed that their presence in the village was now suspected.

Haslehust and Cameron found it advisable to move from one 'safe' place to another because, with the exception of Don Domenico Veronesi himself, their other hosts and friends, though scared, couldn't resist the temptation to boast that they were sheltering escaped British officers, thus indicating how brave they were. Such pride, not surprisingly, was liable to land them or others eventually in front of a firing squad.

Beniamino Veronesi was a miller, and it was he who had kept them supplied with bread at his brother's in Fosse. When they had been about a week in Lugo, they received the news for which they had been waiting. The Partisans had found a means of getting them across the River Po, which was the first major obstacle to be negotiated on their way south and was by no means easy to cross without travel papers and a good command of Italian.

The idea was for a man from the Vicenza district, called Vittorio Fantenelli, to guide them down into Verona, where he would lead them to the driver of a wood lorry, in which they would be concealed in the load and driven over a bridge across the Po. Fanteneli visited them in Lugo to issue final instructions as to where they were to meet him. He was unusually blond for an Italian, which despite his Italian name perhaps pointed to some Austrian ancestry – the South Tirol having been part of the Austrian Empire until 1918, when it was handed over to the Italians as a reward for having been on the winning side on that occasion. He told them to climb up to a *malga* and spend the night there, in readiness to walk down to a certain point on the way to Verona and meet him the next day.

It was now mid-December and, though the winter snow hadn't yet arrived, the *malga* would have been very cold if they hadn't managed to get a good fire going to warm them. They survived the night and duly kept their rendezvous with Vittorio Fantenelli the next morning.

The descent to Verona went without a hitch and when they reached the flat area on the northern outskirts of the city, Fantenelli led them on to a tram. They were glad of the rest, but the journey to the centre of the city produced one moment of tension. After a couple of stops, a German *Feldwebel* boarded the tram and stood in the centre, strap-hanging. The two escapers and their escort were seated on a side bench, facing the centre. Immediately opposite them sat a couple of teen-age girls, who seemed very curious about the travellers opposite them. They began to nudge each other and to giggle. Finally one of them could contain herself no longer and, pointing to Desmond's brown cut-down boots, whispered to her friend: *Inglesi!* Luckily the German was facing the other way and Desmond was able to catch the girl's eye and put a finger to his lips. This had the desired effect of silencing the girls and stopping their giggling before they drew the German's attention to his fellow-passengers.

By the time they reached the city centre, it was late afternoon and they hurried off to meet the lorry-driver who was to ferry them across

Don Domenico Veronesi, Roman Catholic priest at Fosse from 1932 until he died in 1983, at the age of ninety-eight.

(*Left*) Beniamino Verones[i] miller and brother of Don Domenico Veronesi, with s[ome] (but by no means all) of his children in Lugo.

(*Below*) The village of Foss[a in] the hills to the north of Verc[...] with the Corno d'Acquiglio (1545 m.) above it.

the Po. They hadn't gone far, however, before the three of them were surrounded and seized by a posse of eight German soldiers and were securely held with their hands behind their backs. They were bundled off to an old fort in the city, which was now being used as a prison, and a very forbidding and insanitary edifice it proved. Vittorio Fantenelli protested volubly at this rough treatment, but when they reached the inside of the prison the two British officers were shoved into a long narrow cell, where there were a dozen other prisoners. Fantenelli wasn't seen again. By now Haslehust and Cameron were convinced that he had led them right into a trap and was probably even now receiving the reward that the Germans were known to be offering for any escaped Allied servicemen whom the Italians cared to betray to them. With hindsight the prisoners felt that Vittorio Fantenelli's blond hair, so untypical of an Italian, should have alerted them to the possibility that he was of Austrian extraction, in an area which until 1918 had been part of the Austrian Empire. This, coupled with the enticement of the bounty on the heads of re-captured Allied prisoners-of-war, could well have accounted for a leaning towards the Germans. Their suspicions mounted, but it was too late now. It was only after the war was over that these suspicions were confirmed, by the news that Fantenelli had been executed by the Partisans for his pro-German activities.

Meanwhile, Haslehust and Cameron found themselves sharing wooden bunks with an assorted collection of prisoners, together with plenty of bed-bugs and lice. Food was minimal and sanitation was by means of a revolting communal bucket in the cell. Once a day the prisoners were allowed out into a yard, with a human manure heap in the middle, to which those who felt inclined could add their public contribution.

In the cell, which was at the top of a tower, Desmond Haslehust got into conversation with two of the other inmates. One was a friendly Franciscan friar who had been imprisoned for helping escaped prisoners-of-war, and the other was an Admiral in the Italian navy who was implicated in the handing over of much of the Italian fleet to the Allies at La Spezia at the time of the armistice. Haslehust and Cameron regarded him as an arrant coward, because when they proposed knotting some blankets together to make an improvised rope with which to let themselves down to the dry moat round the fort,

after they had managed to open the cell door, he said that he would
be liable to unpleasant reprisals from the guards if he didn't raise
the alarm, if anybody escaped. Therefore, if they started anything,
he would be obliged to raise the alarm and inform the guards. So
that was the end of that plan.

Haslehust and Cameron's next move was to complain about their
filthy conditions, invoking the Geneva Convention – a ploy that had
met with spasmodic success in Italian POW camps. For two weeks
nothing happened and the conditions remained atrocious. Christmas
1943 came and went amid these grisly unfestive surroundings, leaving
their spirits at a low ebb. Eventually they were carted off to a large
house not far away, which was being used as a Gestapo headquarters.
Here they were to face their first Gestapo interrogation.

They were brought before a middle-aged German officer in uniform,
with an expressionless face and cold cod-fish eyes. Before the
interrogation began, they were stripped naked. They were pushed
and slapped, but not at this stage beaten up or tortured. The main
object seemed to be frighten and humiliate them. The interrogator
told them to explain who and what they were. He brushed aside their
assertions that they were escaped prioners-of-war and their claim that
they should be treated as such. They were asked for the names of
the people who had aided them, and when this information was not
forthcoming, despite threats and manhandling of increasing intensity,
the interrogator lost patience and declared that they were obviously
spies and would be shot the next morning.

They were given their clothes back and were bundled off to a room
used as a cell, with a cold cement floor, devoid of any furniture or
beds. All they could do was sit on the floor and contemplate their
fate – which their present surroundings, with no food or water for
twenty-four hours, gave them little reason to doubt. Strangely enough,
they were both so exhausted from their ordeal that, far from having
a sleepless night, they soon dropped off to sleep on the bare hard floor.
In fact when the guards came for them in the morning, they had to
be woken up to face their expected execution.

Resigned to being shot, they were led out into a courtyard and made
to face the wall. It all seemed very final, but no firing-party arrived.
Instead, an escort of German guards appeared and marched them
off to a truck which was waiting outside. They were ordered to climb

into the back and were driven off to an unknown destination. This turned out to be a POW camp at Modena, where they had first boarded the train for Innsbruck three months previously, before all their wanderings. There they joined other prisoners awaiting transport to Germany. Some were recently captured in the fighting in the south; others were re-captured escapers like themselves. It was both a disappointment and a relief to be back with the status of prisoner-of-war, with their own kind, without the strain of having to talk Italian.

So ended an escape which had begun three months earlier and, despite much friendly help from Italians in the mountains, had ended in betrayal in Verona, not far from their starting-point. At least they had tasted freedom for a while – and mercifully they were still alive.

\*

With Desmond Haslehust and John Cameron once more behind barbed-wire, it is time to return to Tug Wilson and see where his bid for freedom took him after he vanished from Modena station before the train departed.

# CHAPTER 18

# Rome Express

When Tug Wilson walked out of Modena station, clad in overalls provided by the friendly Italian railwayman, he followed his rescuer to a nearby railwayman's cottage, adjoining the station yard. The cottage stood on a small plot of ground and Tug was directed to an empty rabbit-hutch in which he was to hide, while the man went off to fetch help. Tug quickly did as the man indicated and lay there, trying to keep silent, but his heart was beating almost audibly, as he wondered what would happen.

He felt fairly sure that the Italian was friendly and reliable, because all the Italian railway-workers whom they had encountered in the station had left little doubt in the minds of the prisoners as to where their sympathies lay. Following the fall of Mussolini and the recent armistice they now appeared to be firmly on the side of the Allies and clearly disenchanted with their former comrades-in-arms, the Germans. It seemed unlikely that, having so neatly extricated Tug from the train, the man would now hand him over to the Germans. In any case he had little alternative but to take this risk. If he attempted to run away, where would he run to?

Then, with his heart still thumping, he heard a sound that was music to his ears. He heard the slow chugging of an engine gradually getting up steam and leaving the station. It could only be his train, he reckoned. He had left it just in time.

Now he had to wait and, after about half an hour of relief that the train had gone without him, which gave way to anxiety about his next move, he heard footsteps and voices approaching his rabbit-hutch. He looked out of his primitive hiding-place and saw his original helper arriving back in company with a youngish man and a woman with a baby in her arms. The young couple beckoned him to follow them and, to his initial dismay, he was handed the baby to carry. He soon discovered the reason behind this sensible move when they reached a cross-roads with a German tank parked right across it. Tug kept walking nonchalantly along, doing his best to look fatherly. This camouflage took them safely past the German tank, the inmates of which paid no attention to the 'Italian' father carrying the inevitable bambino. Soon they came to a public swimming-pool surrounded by a high fence and, somewhat to Tug's surprise, they turned into the enclosure through a side-entrance. He was taken straight to a kitchen attached to the pool restaurant and given some food. There to his further surprise and delight he met another escaper from the same train – a fair-haired Royal Engineers captain called Ivor Roworth who had been captured early in 1943 in Tunisia. Between them they had only a smattering of Italian but, with the aid of explanatory gestures, they began to make themselves understood. They explained that they wanted to escape south to join the Allied troops who would soon be arriving.

They were taken by the same young couple to a house in Modena, Number 80 Via Gadeceto. Here they were told that they would be billeted for a few days, pending arrangements for passing them on to some organisation. They were directed to a double bed which they were to share and were told that they were not to go outside or be seen, because there were Germans billeted in the same street.

Here they lived for sixteen days. They were fed by their hosts, a middle-aged Italian couple, Signor Mario Lugli and his wife and were encouraged to learn a little more Italian, chiefly, it seemed, for the amusement that it caused when they uttered any. Though the Italians were unmistakeably friendly and hospitable, they were also understandably nervous. They said that they were in touch with an organisation that helped escaped prisoners-of-war. But first the two officers needed some civilian clothes and identity cards, to enable them to travel and pass themselves off as Italian civilians, should they be stopped on a train or in the street.

First they were each given a hat, trousers, shirts, shoes, a tie and a light overcoat. A couple of days later they were provided with some lire and identity cards. Tug's was in the name of Signor Alberto Villani, of the Agricultural and Forestry Department in Sicily. Since Sicily had by now been over-run by the enemy, there would be no chance of checking the records there – and of course many Sicilians had managed to flee the island.

When they were thus equipped for travel they were warned to be ready to leave on a night train from Modena station. Members of the organisation would call for them, escort them to the train and travel with them on their journey.

When the escort arrived to fetch them, the two officers found that they were in the hands of two middle-aged Roman Catholic priests in black clerical dress. The party set off straight for Modena station – from which the two officers had been only too glad to escape a week previously. But now, instead of heading unwillingly towards the Brenner Pass in a cattle-truck en route for further indefinite imprisonment in Germany, they were installed in a second-class carriage about to head in the opposite direction. They were now bound for Rome, which would be a big step on their way south to meet the Allied forces that had landed in southern Italy and were thought to be advancing northwards – though reliable news had been hard to come by. At all events it was a good feeling to be on their way south.

One of the priests had bought tickets for all of them and they had managed to find seats, in pairs, each priest escorting one escaper. The train was crowded with civilians and German and Italian soldiers in uniform. It seemed that at that chaotic time in Italy everybody was trying to move to somewhere else. But there also seemed to be no hindrance to travellers, such as searches or checks on identity. A month later it was to prove a vastly different matter, when the Fascist police, reverting to a policy of collaborating with the Germans, began to re-establish their control on the movement of civilians. It later became very difficult to circulate in Italy by train, unless one could produce the necessary documents. But now, in late September, in the aftermath of the Armistice between Italy and the Allies, the situation was still fluid and travel, though crowded, was relatively trouble-free. Controls and arrests were to come in the near future for unwary or unlucky travellers.

The journey through the night began at about 10 p.m. Already it was dark and the two escaped prisoners could, with every justification, feign and ultimately achieve a sound sleep. Naturally they didn't dare get into conversation with anyone – not even their escorts. It was safer to sleep. In any case they could see nothing out of the window, as they sped through the night. The train appeared to be an express and travelled at a fast speed through the darkness. The sensation reminded Tug of his journeys in submarines, travelling as it were in a capsule through the dark ocean. He just sat back and relaxed, trusting to Fate.

His one moment of panic was caused by his own carelessness – of the kind that has cost more than one escaper his freedom. When he stepped past a German soldier in his carriage, in order to go to the lavatory during the night, he started to say 'Sorry' in English. Even as he started to say it he managed to swallow his word in time and blurt out *'Scusate, Signor, per favore!'* To most Germans, Italian with an English accent was indistinguishable from the genuine thing, and the German merely nodded acceptance of the garbled apology. This small incident served to put Tug on his guard for the future.

Early the next morning the express train pulled into Rome's main station. Waiting at the barrier was another priest, a large friendly-looking man, who was there to receive the two ex-prisoners and take charge of them. As they were soon to discover, he was the organiser of the Rome escape-line, which was about to develop into a vast concern with wide ramifications.

He was a remarkable man – Monsignor O'Flaherty, by name, and Irish by nationality.

# CHAPTER 19

# Vatican Scuffle

The Right Reverend Monsignor Hugh O'Flaherty was a six-feet-three Irishman, with grey hair brushed back from his forehead forming a widow's peak at the front, with the sides kept short. He wore glasses, above which there were well-defined eyebrows. He had a kindly cheerful face and a determined chin. By virtue of his neutral citizenship he was free to wander in Rome and further afield and, having been there since 1922, he was widely known in the capital. What was more he was widely liked. He was by no means enamoured of the British, but his antipathy in that direction was swept aside by a revulsion against the Nazis and Fascists after their treatment of Jews and non-Fascists and other victims of their displeasure.

Strangely enough, this meeting with Monsignor O'Flaherty was not Tug's first glimpse of this remarkable priest. The Monsignor had first come into contact with Allied prisoners-of-war in 1941, when he was appointed secretary-interpreter to the Papal Nuncio, whom he accompanied on tours of POW camps all over central and northern Italy. It was on a visit to Sulmona camp to see what could be done to ease the plight of the prisoners (which was a step in the right direction as far as the prisoners were concerned, even if the benefits weren't always noticeable or immediate) that Monsignor O'Flaherty first appeared on Tug Wilson's horizon. This was early in 1943. A group of prisoners, including Tug, managed to get near the Monsignor and asked him when he thought the war in Italy might be over and they would be freed. His reply, with an Irish lilt, was: 'By the Grace of God and the Favour of the Apostolic See – by the end of the year'. This oracular reply stuck in Tug's mind and, by the Grace of God (and doubtless the Favour of the Apostolic See as well), here he was in the care of the priest who had uttered it. The war wasn't yet over in Italy – far from it, as it turned out – but at least Tug was no longer languishing in a prisoner-of-war camp, and he dared to hope that he was on his way to re-join the Allied forces further south.

Monsignor O'Flaherty welcomed his new arrivals – for he had received many others before – with a Red Cross parcel, obtained from the Swiss Legation with which he was in constant touch, to be shared between them, accompanied by some German cigars. He came by the latter because he lived and worked in the Collegio Teutonicum, which was adjacent to but not actually part of the Vatican City. It was what was known as extra-territorial property, belonging to the Holy See and not forming part of the Italian state. The German College was served largely by devout German nuns, who looked after the Monsignor. So far it had suffered no interference from the Wehrmacht since the occupation of Rome on 12th September, nor had the Gestapo seen fit to raid it. The Monsignor was still allowed to come and go as he pleased, the College having direct access to the streets of Rome.

To the surprise and initial unease of the two escaped officers, Monsignor O'Flaherty led them brazenly through the centre of Rome. There was to be no scuttling down side streets for them – in fact the Monsignor seemed intent on showing his 'tourists' the sights of the Holy City! They were led into St Peter's Square, past the Vatican and even had the Pope's window pointed out to them. Then they realised why they were being led this way – Monsignor O'Flaherty was delivering them to a safe billet that he had found for them near St Peter's Square.

Tug Wilson and Ivor Roworth were taken to the home of an obviously well-to-do Italian family. The owner, Signor Rulli, lived there with his wife and two daughters, and employed a housemaid. They were friends of Monsignor O'Flaherty and their house was one of the numerous billets to which the priest could take the ever-increasing numbers of escaped prisoners-of-war who were converging on Rome and its surroundings. The two priests who had collected Wilson and Roworth from Modena were part of Monsignor O'Flaherty's escape-line. He had several other helpers, and the two officers had fallen into very good hands – a just reward for their own initiative in escaping.

Safely installed in their billet, the two men were well looked after. For the present they were ordered to stay indoors, off the streets of Rome. Apparently this was to be merely a temporary billet, to be used until a more secure hide-out could be arranged.

When the time came for the two escapers to be moved, Tug Wilson was ordered to shave off his military moustache and both of them were provided with priests' soutanes to put over their other clothes for the move. They were escorted by another priest to what was considered to be a very safe billet in the Via Firenze, which leads off the Via Venti Settembre, which housed many of the larger Ministry buildings – akin to Whitehall in London. The area was cordoned off at night on account of a high-ranking German general in a hotel in the block. This made the sector safe from snap raids by the German or Italian police at night, which were becoming increasingly frequent elsewhere in the city. The area was consequently comparatively quiet. By day the two men, both equipped with Italian clothes and identity papers, were now allowed out for exercise.

The two escaped prisoners now felt reasonably secure from re-arrest and had time to take stock of their situation. Should they lie low where they were until the Allies arrived, or should they make a bid to work their way further south under their own steam to cross the line to their own troops? Many had attempted to adopt this plan but some had had to turn back, and not much was known about the fate of the others. The going was getting tougher as winter approached and the hills became covered in snow, and the German defence-lines stiffened, making the areas immediately behind them increasingly hazardous to cross.

Another possibility was to attempt to reach either the Adriatic or the Tyrrhenian coast and make the journey south by boat. There was, indeed talk of such schemes, some reputedly successful and others ending in betrayal and capture. In any case Tug Wilson and Ivor Roworth had no contacts to launch them on any coastal ventures. On balance it seemed wisest to stay put and wait a bit longer.

Monsignor O'Flaherty's escape organisation, which had grown out of all manageable proportions, now had a remarkable British Gunner officer in charge, Major Sam Derry by name. He had himself entered Rome beneath a pungent pile of cabbages in the back of a peasant's cart. He had managed to leap from a Germany-bound train from Sulmona, whither he had been taken in company with the occupants of Chieti camp, where an even worse debacle had occurred than at Bologna, following the armistice on 8th September 1943.

On arrival in Rome, concealed under a cart-load of reeking

cabbages past the check-point, Major Derry had been directed to Monsignor O'Flaherty's room in the Collegio Teutonicum. There he was installed and passed off as an Irish writer, staying with the Monsignor and being fed by the dutiful German nuns, who were well-disposed towards their 'Irish' guest. From here Derry was guided by the Monsignor into the nearby Vatican, disguised in one of O'Flaherty's spare soutanes – the two men being most conveniently of equal height – to meet the British Minister in the Vatican City, who was operating there with a skeleton staff.

The Minister was a man of sixty, Sir D'Arcy Osborne, a polished imperturbable diplomat to his finger-tips. Major Sam Derry was the very man he had been looking for. He was the first escaped prisoner-of-war of field-officer rank with whom the Minister had made contact. Sir D'Arcy Osborne quickly sized up his man, liked what he saw, and asked him to run the Rome Organization for coping with escaped Allied prisoners of all nationalities – a request that Major Derry felt bound to accept. The escape line which Monsignor O'Flaherty and his fellow priests and other helpers had been running on their own had now been swamped by the sudden influx of escapers from far and wide, who needed receiving, guiding, checking, hiding, clothing and feeding – and all this required an officer of outstanding organising ability and drive.

But this appointment was not confirmed until the Minister had made some very full enquiries about Derry's bona fides and background, through the War Office, Scotland Yard and even from his father in Newark, Nottinghamshire. Security was never Monsignor O'Flaherty's strong point, but the Minister was not a man to run unwarranted risks.

To carry out his task, Derry's pressing need was going to be funds to help pay the *padroni*, as the hosts were called, for the maintenance of the ex-prisoners-of-war lodged in their houses and flats. This was where the shrewd brain and persuasive manner of Sir D'Arcy Osborne came into the picture. Via neutral Lisbon he was able to induce the release of British Government money in various ways for the maintenance of stranded ex-prisoners-of-war or evaders on the run and the *padroni* who so gallantly harboured them, in spite of the very real threats of death for doing so.

This money was delivered at fairly regular invervals by a team of helpers, of whom none were more active and resourceful than two former inmates of Chieti camp whom Derry had known and liked, John Furman and Bill Simpson, both Lieutenants in the Royal Artillery. They had already proved their resourcefulness by reaching Rome following separate daring escapes, and now they were to prove invaluable to Derry and his Rome Organisation, as it became known – though its existence could not be bruited abroad at the time. Funds had to be distributed not only in Rome but to groups of ex-prisoners who had gone to ground in outlying farm areas for miles around, and a few much further afield than that. It wasn't safe to allow too great a concentration in Rome itself, and it was the organisation's policy to keep groups and individuals provided for outside the city as well as inside its boundaries. To such an extent did the organisation expand that, by the time the long-awaited Allied troops finally reached Rome, on 4th June 1944, there were on the books of the Rome organisation no less than 3,925 escapers and evaders of many Allied nationalities – Britishers, South Africans, Greeks, Russians and Americans. In pursuance of Derry's policy of dispersal, only 200 of these were billeted actually in Rome itself.

Thanks to the Rome Organisation Tug Wilson and Ivor Roworth were able to subsist in reasonable comfort – as long as their billet remained safe. But therein lay their first problem.

There were unsettling rumours that their billet was now under observation from the Gestapo, and they began to wonder whether it would be wiser to attempt to gain entry into the Vatican, where they would be interned until the Allies captured Rome. Meanwhile, of course, they would be safe from re-arrest. Tug regarded this as something of a dead end and was not in favour of the idea, especially as it was known that since the armistice the Vatican had closed its doors to the sudden rush of escaped prisoners-of-war who sought refuge there. The Swiss guards had been instructed to turn away all who applied for admission through the gates.

Then one day there was a sudden knock at the door of the house where they were billeted in the Via Firenze and, as always before opening, Roworth looked through the key-hole and saw, to his horror, the buckle of a German soldier's belt. Without answering the door, he and Tug immediately dropped down from the back window into the courtyard of the Anglo-American church and walked into the Via Nazionale.

With Roworth leading the way and Tug still feeling a bit hesistant about the idea of trying to enter the Vatican, the two officers made their way in that direction. The Germans had mounted a twenty-four hour guard round the Vatican, as a gesture of respect for its neutrality. Roworth and Wilson managed to walk past this cordon, only to come up against the Swiss guards at the entrance. They were stopped and questioned, whereupon Roworth darted inside, leaving Tug Wilson alone with the angry Swiss guards who, after a scuffle, evicted him. He dodged between the colonnades to safety outside, fortunately without drawing the attention of the outer cordon of German sentries, who luckily were facing outwards.

Roworth remained inside the Vatican, after his opportunist entry and was duly interned. This, however, didn't prevent him from doing useful work for the Rome Organisation from inside the city. He was obliged, of course, to remain interned there until the arrival of the Allies in June 1944.

Tug Wilson, meanwhile, returned cautiously to his billet and there found that the coast was clear before entering. But even though it had been a false alarm, he thought it expedient to find another billet without delay. With the help of the Organisation he moved to his third billet in Rome, No 3 Via Guiseppe Palumbo, to a modern flat on the sixth floor. The owner of the flat was Signor Nebulante, who came originally from Florence. This was thought to be a safe billet and Tug settled down to an undisturbed existence. His host Nebulante taught him Italian and Tug visited some other prisoners in less affluent quarters, delivering funds on behalf of the Rome Organisation.

When Monsignor O'Flaherty heard of Tug Wilson's scuffle with the Vatican guards who ejected him, he was most upset – as indeed was Tug at the time. O'Flaherty offered to try to get him into the Vatican, with the possibility of an audience with the Pope, in an attempt to redress matters. But by then Tug was nicely re-settled in Nebulante's flat and told O'Flaherty not to worry any further about the incident.


At about this time, in November 1943, Tug was asked if he minded having another officer, for whom the Organisation was seeking

accommodation, sent to join him in Via Giuseppe Palumbo. Tug
readily agreed and was delighted when the new arrival turned out
to be someone with whom he was to get on very well – Captain Philip
(Pip) Gardner, VC, MC, who had escaped from his prison camp
following the Italian armistice of 8th September and had made his
way to Rome.

Captain Pip Gardner had been a Territorial with the Westminster
Dragoons before the war and had fought in the Western Desert with
the 4th Royal Tank Regiment in Matilda tanks. He had been
decorated for bravery twice: in May 1941 during the first siege of
Tobruk, when the encircled port held out valiantly, first with
Australian troops, and later with British replacements; he received
the MC for his part in the fighting on the plain below Halfaya Pass,
on the way up to Bardia. Six months later, in November 1941, he
was awarded the VC (the first such honour to be awarded to a Tank
officer in the Desert) in the fighting at El Duda, between Sidi Rezegh
and Tobruk, as the Eighth Army made its successful autumn bid to
drive Rommel's troops back to Benghazi and beyond, albeit only
temporarily, as the Desert campaign ebbed and flowed.

In June 1942, three days after the fall of Tobruk when Rommel
had surrounded it again, Pip Gardner was captured. After General
Klopper's surrender, which landed thousands of dumbfounded troops
in the bag, Gardner set off on foot beyond the defensive perimeter
in company with Brigadier Willison and Colonel Reeves, the
Commander of the 32nd Army Tank Brigade and the CO of the 4th
Royal Tank Regiment respectively. After three days attempting to
escape across the desert on foot, they were rounded up, and Pip's
life as a prisoner-of-war began.

He was flown across the Mediterranean to the Italian prisoner-of-
war transit camp at Bari, which was later the scene of one amusing
incident. New arrivals were placed in a quarantine hut within the
camp. Their only form of exercise was to pace up and down outside
their hut, counter-marching when they reached the barbed-wire at
the end of the enclosure. At that time it was possible to procure packets
of dried figs from the canteen with camp money issued to officers,
against their pay by arrangement through the Red Cross. There was
precious little else that they could buy, but in their hungry state, always
most acute in the early days of captivity before their stomachs had

contracted and adjusted, the prisoners devoured these figs for their sugar content and satisfying bulk – regardless of the inevitable flatulent consequences associated with figs. There were three South African padrés, who had been captured at Tobruk, among those in the quarantine enclosure. They were taking their exercise, and doubtless thinking holy thoughts, when they reached the end of their beat and counter-marched. As they did so, one of them, who had eaten his share of figs, chose this moment to break wind in a most thorough-going manner. Unfortunately an Italian guard was stationed at the wire and caught the full blast of this unholy detonation. The result was a week in the cooler for all three padrés for insulting behaviour to the Italian army – thus providing much comic relief to the rest of the camp!

From Bari, Pip Gardner was sent to Chieti, in central Italy, where he soon became an active tunneller. This pursuit resulted in a transfer to Fontanellato, a much more comfortable camp near Parma in the Lombardy Plain in northern Italy.

After the armistice on 8th September 1943, under the alert leadership of the Senior British Officer, Colonel De Burgh, Fontanellato was one of the few camps where the order to stay put (like sitting ducks) was in part ignored, owing to the altered circumstances since its promulgation through MI9. Colonel De Burgh boldly led his men out of camp in the nick of time, in organised groups, before releasing them in batches (rather than in a disorganised horde) to make their own escapes.

Pip Gardner chose to travel south in order to reach the Allied forces, in company with a great friend from the Westminster Dragoons and the 4th Royal Tank Regiment, Captain 'Percy' Gers – he was really Ronald Gers, but was widely known as 'Percy' because of a similarity in looks to Percy Fender, the well-known Surrey and England cricketer. Partly on foot and partly by bicycle they had arrived at a point ninety miles north of Rome, when the snow descended. They were in hiding there when news of them reached their former fellow-inmate of Chieti, Major Sam Derry. The latter, as organiser of the Rome escape line, had already spread his tentacles well beyond the city and its immediate surroundings. He despatched an Italian partisan who was working for him to fetch Pip from his hide-out in the hills by bus. The courrier could only escort one person at a time and the idea was that Percy Gers would be fetched as soon as possible. In the event it never became possible to fetch him, owing to a series of crises at the Rome end of the over-stretched escape line. Gers, however, to his great credit, managed eventually to make his own way south to reach the Allied lines.

Pip's journey to Rome lasted seven hours, during which time he had to feign illness as an excuse for not speaking throughout the entire journey. On arrival in Rome, he was directed by Sam Derry to Signor Nebulante's flat where he was accommodated with Tug Wilson.

Pip Gardner was dark-haired, of medium height and build, and very alert. He was in his late twenties, and thus a couple of years younger than Tug. Like the latter, he too was married, and they clicked from the start. Between them these two highly decorated officers constantly tried to think of ways out of Rome by going southwards to the Allied lines, which were advancing depressingly slowly towards them, in the face of stiff German resistance and the onset of winter snows which had followed the mud and slush of autumn.

Tug Wilson and Pip Gardner were well-equipped with Italian civilian clothing and identity cards, to which were added season tickets on the buses – all provided by their hosts and through the Rome Organisation. Neither man was the type to mope around morosely in the flat, nor to slink furtively down side-streets. With cash provided by the Rome Organisation they frequently went to cafés for coffee and brandy – and a change of scenery. One day, however, their confidence was briefly shaken. The owner of a café which they often frequented suddenly pointed a pistol at them and said '*Mani in alto!*' (Hands up!). Cold shivers ran down their spines, until the man revealed that it was only a wooden pistol. He was having a joke at their expense, as he knew that they were *Inglesi*. Tug and Pip survived the 'joke'!

To relieve the boredom, two Yugoslav girls whom they had met in Nebulante's flat, who were keen opera-goers, arranged for Tug to Pip to accompany them to the opera House for a performance of *La Traviata*, sung by Beniamino Gigli and his daughter Rina. On the way home from the opera, they were standing in a bus with the two girls when one of the latter, carried away for a moment and forgetting where they were, suddenly said in loud English: 'That was an excellent opera. Did you enjoy it?' Fortunately this unguarded utterance was

Oflag 79 at Brunswick, Germany, in 1944 before the last lean winter of the war. The group includes British, South African and New Zealand officers, with Pip Gardner and Tug Wilson seated on the ground in the centre of the front row.

Better times. Tug Wilson, DSO and Bar, with Pip Gardner, VC, MC, at a post-war Royal Tank Regiment reunion.

(*Above*) Korea 1952. Major Tug Wilson with his Tactical Headquarters personnel.

(*Left*) Major Tug Wilson in Korea, as battery Commander with the First Field Regiment, Royal Artillery.

lost in the general buzz of conversation to which, even in wartime, Italians are prone. Only when the four opera-goers reached 'home' could they afford to laugh.

Christmas was drawing near and Tug was naturally constantly thinking of his wife Marjorie at home in Bristol. He had had no communication either way since he had escaped at Modena in September, but she was constantly uppermost in his thoughts. As Christmas approached he felt the urge to buy her a present, in the hope that he might soon be in a position to deliver it to her in person. Using some of his precious subsistence allowance from the organisation that he had saved, he went to a shop in the city centre and bought her an attractive solid silver compact, hoping that she would like it. He kept it in his pocket and this compact was to have a strange history, the next two instalments of which will unfold as Tug's own story progresses.

Christmas and New Year came and went in Nebulante's flat. Food and drink was by then getting very scarce in Rome and the seasonal festivities were perforce restricted to an austere minimum. But early in the New Year life in the flat came to an abrupt end. Nebulante told them that his brother-in-law, a communist, had been arrested and put in gaol, and was being beaten up. A man, who turned out to be a Fascist, arrived at Nebulante's flat with the story that he had himself been in gaol with Nebulante's brother-in-law. Over lunch, to which Nebulante rashly invited this man, to the displeasure and apprehension of Tug and Pip, he explained that there was a plan to spring the brother-in-law from gaol. The plan was to involve Tug Wilson and Pip Gardner and they were to be briefed further.

Next day, 8th January 1944, two plain clothes Gestapo men burst into the flat with Lugers in their hands and made Tug, Pip and Nebulante stand on a settee and put their hands high above them against the wall. Thinking that they had rounded up a hot-bed of Italian communists, they pushed and kicked them roughly. At this stage Tug whispered to Pip: 'Let's rush them and get their guns.' Before Pip had time to reply to this suggestion, in rushed six soldiers in SS uniform and proceeded to bundle the three men out of the flat and down to a waiting truck below. The three captives were driven off to the notorious and euphemistically named Regina Coeli (Queen of Heaven) prison, a large forbidding building which dominates the north bank of the River Tiber, not far from the Collegio Teutonicum.

After nearly four months on the loose, Tug's spell of freedom had come to an abrupt end. He was once more securely back in a gaol – of a far more unpleasant kind than he had hitherto experienced.

# CHAPTER 20

# Handcuffs Overboard

Rome's infamous Regina Coeli prison, reputed to be escape-proof, was crammed full of people arrested by the Fascist police and the Gestapo. Together they had been spreading their drag-net in order to gather up as many of Rome's communists as they could scoop. Among the haul they also netted a few escaped prisoners-of-war, whom they duly detained and questioned. The only hope of those detained of not being shot as communists or spies was to establish their identity as escaped prisoners-of-war. Some who failed to do so were in fact shot.

On arrival at the reception office inside the main gates of the prison, which were shut very firmly behind them, the three newcomers were searched and relieved of any valuables in their possession. Tug lost the compact which he had bought for his wife and was carrying in his pocket, as well as a small sum of lire. Fortunately he had no incriminating papers or addresses on him, which would have put the Rome Organisation in peril.

The three men were put into separate cells on different floors, so that they should have no further contact with each other. Tug found himself in with three other prisoners. He shared the cell with two Italians and an unfortunate Russian Jew. The latter was one of the most pathetic creatures that Tug had ever met. He had already suffered badly at the hands of the Gestapo and was now a broken man – bereft of all resistance and devoid of hope. His expectation of life, in his own estimation and doubtless quite realistically, was virtually nil. The two Italians, on the other hand, were as cheerful as circumstances would allow and were decidedly friendly towards the British officer in their midst.

The cell was cramped and filthy, the filth emanating from a lavatory bucket in one corner, which could only be slopped out each morning, regardless of whether it needed emptying more often. This was a chore which the two Italians absolutely refused to let a British officer perform,

*BEYOND THE BRENNER PASS*

despite Tug's offers to do it. The food was brought once a day, consisting of a vile sort of soup or skilly and a tiny roll of bread. Furthermore, Rome was in the grip of an abnormally hard winter and the cold added to the prisoners' tribulations.

For several days Tug endured these grim conditions, waiting for the inevitable interrogation on the outcome of which his fate would depend. He hadn't been able to contact Pip Gardner or Nebulante, but one day when he insisted on taking his turn at emptying the slop-pail he caught a brief glimpse of something which sickened and upset him badly. He saw his former *padrone*, Nebulante, who was a Resistance leader and had already been roughly treated as such, dragging himself along the passage with great difficulty. He had obviously been beaten up to such an extent that he could no longer walk upright. He had clearly been interrogated and the sight of him in this battered state did little to cheer the prospect of Tug's own interrogation, which was bound to come. Yet despite his increased apprehension, he knew that he must undergo questioning if he were to establish his true identity as an escaped British officer. He just hoped he could get it over soon.

When he was finally called for interrogation he was led to an interview room and brought before a Gestapo officer who, to Tug's relief, proved to be by no means offensive. He seemed prepared to accept from the start that Tug was indeed a British officer. He seemed delighted with his bonus catch of a British officer in his round-up of Italian communists. Tug was returned unharmed and more than a little relieved to his cell, where all he could do was sit and await developments.

On one occasion Tug Wilson and Pip Gardner were able to shout a few words of encouragement to each other from their cells, despite being on different floors. Amid the general hubbub it was difficult to establish contact. But one day when they tried to do so, a voice shouted: '*Silenzio – lascia' parlare gli Inglesi!*' (Silence – let the Englishmen speak!). Quite remarkably six or seven hundred prisoners were hushed to let Tug and Pip exchange a few words of greeting to each other.

When news of the Anzio bridgehead reached the inside of the prison, some of the German guards were withdrawn for a short while, and the remainder of them thought that the Allied troops would soon be in Rome. So for that matter did the prisoners. But the guards were soon replaced by others.

The arrest of Tug and Pip had led to another swoop the same day, which netted two more British officers, one of Major Derry's right-hand men, Lieutenant John Furman, and the organisation's RAMC doctor, Captain Macauley. Their arrest came about as the result of that of Nebulante with Tug and Pip. The Gestapo had taken Nebulante's cook, a small white-haired old man, and frightened him into leading them to another of the organisation's flats, in Via Chelini. The cook knew the secret signal that had to be given on the doorbell before it would be opened. In this manner the two plain-clothes Gestapo men gained access and in no time they called in their uniformed SS men and had the occupants, a Yugoslav communist and an Austrian girl as well as the two British officers, lined up against a wall with their hands held high above their heads. The Gestapo were cock-a-hoop with another good catch.

Though Tug Wilson heard that John Furman was being held on the same floor in Regina Coeli, he never managed to see him or make contact with him. But Furman managed to get a message out of the gaol to Major Derry, which was smuggled out by an Italian barber who was allowed inside the prison to shave the prisoners, who weren't allowed to use their own razors. The message confirmed that Gardner and Wilson were still being held in the gaol. Furman also gave the names of four other officers and six other ranks being detained there. His note was dated 23rd January 1944, fifteen days after Tug's arrest. Furman sent another note two days later, saying that all the British prisoners were about to leave in two or three hours time. Tug was on his way to Germany.

The first part of Tug's journey northwards, bound for Germany, was by coach under heavily-armed escort, after dire warnings as to the consequences of any attempts to escape in transit. They were driven ninety miles to a staging camp at Pissignano, near Spoleto and south of Florence. Here they were added to another assembly of prisoners, some of them captured in the fighting of recent weeks and others, like Tug and Pip, recaptured after being at large. Two days later they were put into cattle-trucks and began a long, hungry, tedious and cheerless journey up to the Brenner Pass.

Since the early days of cattle-truck travel for prisoners-of-war being transfered from Italy to Germany, dating from September 1943, experience had taught the Germans that escapes could be much reduced by the removal of the prisoners' boots, especially now that winter had arrived. This now happened to Tug Wilson and Pip Gardner and their party.

It was nearly five months since Tug had first escaped the dreaded journey northwards to Germany, by disappearing from the train at Modena station, and now he was inexorably on his way once more to further captivity. It was a chilling thought. Whereas in September the heat in the cattle-trucks had been stifling, now in the depth of winter the prisoners had to undergo an ordeal by cold. Tug was still in the civilian clothing in which he had been re-captured and he completed the journey in a state of torpor – mental as well as physical.

After four cold and hungry days in a cattle-truck, the train pulled into a station in Germany marked 'Mühlberg', on the River Elbe between Dresden and Leipzig, and the weary prisoners were taken to Stalag IVB. Here things looked up after they had been fumigated and de-loused on arrival. They were issued with Red Cross parcels from the camp stores and they were fitted out with battle dress where necessary, before being assigned to a hut with sleeping-bunks.

But next morning Tug Wilson and Pip Gardner and six others were in for a shock. They were ordered to hand back their newly-issued battle-dress and were made to don their civilian clothing once more. They were escorted to a train and were put into ordinary carriages, for a change, for an undisclosed destination. They travelled through the day and the following night, and next morning they arrived at Luckenwalde, which is about sixty miles south of Berlin. They were marched to a forbidding prison, over which there hung an oppressive atmosphere of impending doom for all those who entered – the type of place that made anyone entering wonder if he would ever get out. Tug couldn't help wondering whether this was to be the end of the road for him, as they were led to solitary cells. They were taken out into a courtyard for exercise next day, where they had to walk slowly in a circle, in a long procession with intervals between each prisoner. Absolutely no talking was allowed, and it was a most depressing place to find oneself.

After a few days languishing apprehensively here, Tug was taken before an SS major for interrogation. Apparently his papers had been sent on with him and the SS major, who was reasonably affable, demanded proof that Tug was in fact who he said he was – Captain Wilson of the Royal Artillery and not a communist or a spy. Tug stuck to what he reckoned to be all that he was obliged to divulge – name, rank and number, plus the fact that he was a British officer in the Royal Artillery Survey Regiment. There could be no harm in disclosing the latter, since it was ages since his capture and longer still since he had served in it. But the SS major was insistent that as further proof of his true identity Tug must give some details of the composition of a Survey Regiment. This Tug refused to do. He was given twenty-four hours in which to make up his mind whether to oblige and thereby clear himself of all charges of being a spy.

Tug decided that any details that he could give were sure to be out-of-date by now. After all he hadn't been near a Survey Regiment since 1940 and now, in 1944, there were bound to have been radical changes. He decided to play along with the SS major in a guarded manner.

Next day, as he began to release a few harmless details, he soon found the SS major filling in the gaps for him. He evidently knew at least as much as Tug would tell him, and probably far more. At any rate, the few details that Tug provided were enough to keep the SS major in a good mood and pander to his superiority complex. He accepted Tug's assertion that he was a re-captured prisoner-of-war.

After a week of uncertainty at Luckenwalde, to their great relief Tug Wilson, Pip Gardner and the six others were told that they were to be sent to a prisoner-of-war camp. They were escorted by train and immediately things began to look up. In fact something like a Bank Holiday spirit came over the party, particularly for Tug and Pip. Not only was it good to be together again and able to converse once more, but there was the added bonus of well-disposed guards.

The escort was under the command a German corporal who had worked in a bar in Hamburg before the war and could speak some English – a fact that appeared to make him distinctly pro-British, coupled no doubt with the state of war as far as Germany was concerned! The corporal began by amusing his charges when he imperiously turned out a whole crowd of civilians from a carriage so that his prisoners could sit down, while the people had to stand in the corridor.

They had to stop and change trains at Dresden and the prisoners asked if they might fill a couple of water-bottles that they had with them. The friendly corporal selected Tug and Pip, who were the best-attired in their civilian suits and raincoats, and bade them follow him. They followed him down the platform and through the barrier, which was guarded by police, and were taken into a large buffet, whereupon their 'friend' told a group of people sitting at a table to move so that his 'guests' could sit. He then proceeded to order large mugs of beer. Tug and Pip noticed that the whole crowd in the buffet had gone silent and when they commented on this, the corporal said: 'They think you are Gestapo' – and of course in their raincoats they certainly looked the part. They chuckled as they quaffed their drinks. Having filled their water-bottles with beer, they returned cheerfully to the train.

While waiting on the platform they saw a train full of gloomy-looking soldiers pulling out of the station. Their guards explained that these were reinforcements on their way to the Russian front. It struck Tug as a far cry from the confident singing troops he had seen spearheading the Blitzkrieg into France in 1940. Times had certainly changed!

That evening they reached their destination, which was a genuine prisoner-of-war camp, Oflag VIII F, at Märisch-Trubau in Czecho-Slovakia.

Despite a certain inevitable disappointment, Tug, who had been for over a month deeply concerned about his fate, was relieved to get back his prisoner-of-war status. What was more, he found himself in the most comfortable camp that he had experienced. Märisch-Trubau was a former Czech Military Academy, which had been converted to an Oflag. It was situated on the border between Czecho-Slovakia's two westernmost components, Bohemia and Moravia, to the east of Prague, amid rolling partly wooded country. The local inhabitants were preponderantly Sudetan Germans with a minority of Czechs. The main camp building was four storeys high, with a basement, and was referred to by its inmates as the 'Biscuit Factory'. But it was heated and much more comfortable than prisoners-of-war were accustomed to finding. Indian officers even had their own cookhouse and received special Red Cross parcels containing ingredients for a variety of curries.

To Märisch-Trubau there had been sent many re-captured prisoners, including Captain Desmond Haslehust after his escape five months earlier from the same train from which Tug Wilson had absconded in September 1943 at Modena. Haslehust's spell of freedom had come to an end in the hands of the Gestapo in Verona. Tug soon met some old familiar faces, many of whom had interesting, if ultimately frustrating, adventures to tell. Tug was able to build up his strength somewhat, with a regular weekly issue of Red Cross food parcels. After his wanderings it was both a relief and an anti-climax to resume the routine of a prisoner-of-war camp – especially with the tide of the war in Europe now clearly ebbing away from the Germans.

Above all, after six months without being able to write to or hear from his wife, Marjorie, he now looked forward to re-establishing contact by means of letters sent via the Red Cross. Marjorie for her part had to endure a total gap of nine months without mail before she heard that her husband was safely inside a prisoner-of-war camp once more. Now she would have to sit it out patiently, she reckoned. But would Tug do the same, she wondered?

Winter turned to spring and the snow on the camp circuit melted. As ever with the arrival of milder weather, the prisoners' minds turned to the chances of escaping. But before Tug could get involved with any schemes at Märisch-Trubau, the news from the east front was giving rise to further optimism among the prisoners as the Russian army pushed towards the Balkans. The Germans, ever anxious to hold on to their prisoners, quickly decided to move the officers of Oflag VIII F from Märisch-Trubau to a safer distance from the fighting and consign them to Oflag 79 at Brunswick (Braunschweig), which is about thirty-five miles to the east of Hanover, in the direction of Berlin.

The prisoners were moved in two batches, the first of which included Tug Wilson and left on 28th April 1944. The journey started off cheerfully enough, with the prisoners singing on their way to the station – partly to cheer themselves up and partly to present a buoyant image to the local inhabitants, who for their part had precious little to sing about at that stage of the war. But the journey itself was not an ordeal to be taken lightly.

Once again they were marched to a long line of cattle-trucks, but for this journey the travelling arrangements had been altered. They were first relieved of their boots and then handcuffed, before being put into one third of the area of each truck, behind barbed wire at one end – eighteen to a truck. In this section there were five benches provided: two along the sides, one across the end and two up the centre. The prisoners were able to hang most of their impedimenta from the roof of the truck, in which there was very little room to move.

The rest of each truck was occupied by guards and their menacing Alsatian dogs. The guards had a table in their section of the truck, under which the sacks containing the prisoners' boots were stacked.

The handcuffs added to the discomfort, but in most trucks there were one or two 'old lags', to whom they were no novelty and not much of a problem. Shortly after the Dieppe raid, when, it was claimed, German prisoners were handcuffed together during the Canadian assault on that port in August 1942, Hitler had ordered as a reprisal that some British prisoners-of-war be handcuffed. Shattering though the announcement must have been at the time to prisoners, many of whom had already been subjected to varied hardships since their capture in 1940, it took little time for an easy way to be found of unlocking the handcuffs. The reprisal gradually fizzled out. Now, as soon as it was dark and the guards couldn't see what was happening, the officers in Tug's truck and several others were able to remove their handcuffs.

When morning came, someone had a bright idea. As the train travelled along through the countryside, an officer beckoned to a guard and indicated that the communal pee-bucket was dangerously full and needed emptying. It was passed carefully through the barbed-wire door to the co-operative guard. He opened the sliding truck-door and without hesitation slung the contents of the bucket through the gap. Out splashed the unwanted urine, together with a whole lot of handcuffs which had found their way to the bottom of the pail. Despite the fact that the handcuffs were now irretrievably overboard, no reprisals were taken. It wasn't the sort of thing that the guards would be keen to report to the officer in charge, at the risk of a stern rebuke for negligence!

The journey continued for two days and two nights until on 1st May they reached their new camp, Oflag 79 at Brunswick. The newcomers found themselves at a large established camp and a few days later they were joined by the second batch from Märisch-Trubau.

It was round about this time that news filtered through of the murder of fifty of the escapers from a tunnel at Stalag Luft III at Sagan. This was naturally a source of great shock and outrage to would-be escapers, but almost immediately some much better news was received – the D-Day landings in Normandy on 6th June 1944.

There followed what seemed a long hiatus to prisoners-of-war, who waited impatiently for every news bulletin – both from the Oberkommando of the Wehrmacht, which was broadcast daily in the camp, and the much more eagerly-awaited version of events from the BBC, which was gathered on the camp's secret radio. But when at last the Americans broke out at Avranches and the battle suddenly became fluid, and Paris fell to the Allies on 25th August 1944, spirits in Brunswick camp were sky high and many talked of being home by Christmas. There seemed no earthly point in trying to escape now. Liberation was surely at hand. But when the Allied action at Arnhem failed to open up the way into Germany itself for an early end to the war, the prisoners of Brunswick and in camps all over central Germany realised that they were in for another winter's wait – and a very hungry wait it was going to prove. For camps near airfields or big cities, as was Oflag 79 at Brunswick, there was the added risk of being hit by Allied bombs – American by day and British by night.

Brunswick camp suffered its first bomb damage on 24th August 1944, during an American daylight raid on the nearby airfield. Bombs fell in the camp and resulted in the deaths of three officers, with eight others seriously wounded and thirty slightly hurt. One German officer and several German soldiers were also killed. There were numerous bomb-craters in the compound, which later filled up with water.

On 14th October there was another raid, on the town of Brunswick, and in the period from 2nd February to 31st March 1945, as the bombing of Berlin worked up to a crescendo, there was an air-raid warning every day or night – or both. Not only did the bombing severely tax the nerves of the prisoners, but the German railway system received such a pounding that the flow of Red Cross parcels was reduced to a mere trickle, which finally dried up completely. The prisoners, who were never anything other than hungry, had to pull in their belts several holes further. Tug Wilson went down from a lean nine-and-a-half stone to a mere eight stone. His backside was near to vanishing point!

However, in this time of adversity, some of the prisoners British and American got together and thought of a scheme which was not only to lift their own morale by causing them to think of others, but was to have an effect which has lasted until this day – and is still continuing. They decided that when (and if) they got home, they would like to start a boys' club. To this end money was raised in the camp to the tune of £13,000. Prisoners-of-war were able to transfer some of their accumulated pay via the Red Cross, and in this way they were able to contribute to such a fund. Among the contributors were Tug Wilson, Pip Gardner and Desmond Haslehust, who have all appeared in this story.

Thus was born the Brunswick Boys' Club, which was started in Fulham, on the advice of the National Association of Boys' Clubs, and was officially opened in 1948 by HRH The Duke of Edinburgh – surely a unique and happy outcome of the prisoners' darkest days.

At last Brunswick camp was liberated by American troops on 12th April 1945, and everyone had to face several more days with little or no rations, until RAF planes arrived to fly them home from Brunswick airfield, the proximity of which had earlier caused the camp to be hit by bombs in error. Tug was flown over Cologne and shown the vast area of desolation and rubble caused by Allied bombers. Then, by way of welcome contrast, his plane landed him safely in the green countryside of Buckinghamshire.

After being dusted with de-lousing powder and fitted out with a few items of clothing at an overnight reception centre, with members of The Women's Volunteer Service in attendance for emergency sewing, Tug was given double food-ration cards and a railway warrant to Bristol, where he found an overjoyed Marjorie waiting for him.

It wasn't long before she found a cushion for him to sit on. He needed it!

# 'As in Duty Bound'

There is a well-worn army slogan, with rather a cynical flavour, to the effect that one should never volunteer for anything – the corollary being that it is better by far to wait and see what Fate has in store. This slogan might have suited a good many soldiers over the years, particularly those with a jaundiced outlook on army life, but it never cut much ice with Tug Wilson. From the very start he was a keen and incurable volunteer.

In 1939 he began by volunteering for the Territorial Army, and it wasn't long before he put his name down for service with the British Expeditionary Force in France. On his return from Dunkirk he very soon volunteered for service with the Commandos, with little real knowledge of what they were in those early days. On his arrival on the Isle of Arran, as soon as he met and talked with Roger Courtney, he volunteered for service with the Folboat Section.

In 1945, after a short period at home to recover from his thin time as a prisoner-of-war, the same volunteering spirit began to surface once more, and it was to continue with him throughout his army career.

Back in Bristol on double rations, in the spring of 1945, Tug began to put on lost weight – not alarmingly, but steadily enough for him to be able to dispense with a cushion to sit on. But he remained lean and spare – as indeed he still is. After three months repatriation leave he was given a very sympathetic posting, which also at long last enabled his wife, Marjorie, to see something of her soldier-husband. Tug was appointed Adjutant of the University of Bristol contingent of the Senior Training Corps, from July to November 1945.

By now he was in the mood once more to volunteer for service abroad – in Palestine, as it was then called, with the 6th Airborne Division ('The Red Devils'). This also involved volunteering for a parachute course, which he completed and passed at Abingdon – quite a transition from going to war in a submarine in the depths of the ocean! Before leaving for Palestine he was summoned to attend a second investiture at Buckingham Palace on 26th February 1946 to receive a Bar to his DSO from His Majesty King George VI, awarded when the full details of his last folboat operation became known. He was delighted to meet Bombardier Brittlebank there, receiving his DCM for the same venture. Tug left for Palestine as battery-commander in the 66th Airborne Anti-Tank Regiment, with the rank of major, where he served until September 1947.

On his return to the United Kingdom he served first as a battery-commander in Heavy Anti-Aircraft and Light Anti-Aircraft and then as Staff Officer Royal Artillery at the Army Air Transport and Development Centre, until the volunteering bug bit him again. This time he volunteered for service in Korea and was there, as well as in Japan, from October 1951 to February 1953, as battery-commander in the 14th Field Regiment, RA, which was the then senior field regiment of the Royal Regiment of Artillery. His return to the United Kingdom was swiftly followed by an announcement in the *London Gazette* of 24th April 1953 of his Mention in Despatches 'in recognition of gallant and distinguished service in Korea' to add to his other decorations.

Back home in Britain, Tug was appointed Second-in-Command of the 38th Training Regiment, RA, in North Wales from June 1953 till March 1956. Though this wasn't an appointment that provided much excitement – he was used to more action – it was an excellent posting which gave him a good grooming for command, under the guidance of Lieutenant-Colonel 'Legs' Lyon. Promotion to a command duly came his way when he volunteered, yet again, for service abroad.

As Commanding Officer of the 37th Heavy Anti-Aircraft Regiment, RA, he and his regiment were shipped in 1956 to Malta for the Suez fiasco, but were not used as this operation fizzled out. The regiment, however, stayed until March 1957 in Malta, the scene of Tug's folboat exploits during the war. This was a landmark in a most unusual career that had begun in the Survey Regiment, RA, of the Territorial Army, and thereafter led him via folboats, submarines, cattle-trucks, prisoner-of-war camps and gaols to further active service with the 6th Airborne Division in Palestine, before taking him, via Korea, to gunnery with the Royal Artillery.

But his volunteering days weren't quite over. He volunteered to take early retirement in order to become Army Careers Officer for Warwickshire, with offices in Coventry, Nuneaton and Warwick. The title of this epilogue – 'As in Duty Bound' – is taken from the Oath of Allegiance, which Tug administered thousands of times, to recruits of all ages and both sexes who joined the army during his fifteen years as Army Careers Officer. It was a uniformed and pensionable appointment which kept him well in touch with the army, but at last allowed him and Marjorie to enjoy a happy and settled married life together.

When he retired in 1973 from his post as Army Careers Officer, Tug became a field officer covering the county of Warwickshire with the Country Landowners Association, which brought him into contact with the local farming community and gave him great pleasure. In 1976, at the age of sixty-five, he retired from work – and from volunteering! Since then he has been able to indulge his long-standing liking for golf. In 1983 he underwent a major abdominal operation from which he made a characteristically determined recovery, which surprised the doctors and himself. As he left the hospital, one of the matrons remarked: 'You certainly are a survivor!' Not the least of

# The Oath of Allegiance

I _____ Swear by Almighty God that I will be faithful and bear true allegiance to Her Majesty Queen Elizabeth the Second, Her Heirs and Successors and that I will as in duty bound honestly and faithfully defend Her Majesty, Her Heirs and Successors, in Person, Crown and Dignity against all enemies and will observe and obey all orders of Her Majesty, Her Heirs and Successors and of the Generals and Officers set over me.

Tug Wilson serving in Palestine in 1946 with the Sixth Airborne Division.

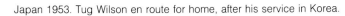

Japan 1953. Tug Wilson en route for home, after his service in Korea.

Lieutenant-Colonel R. Wilson's last recruitment as Army Careers Officer for Warwickshire, on February 23rd 1973. Hair-length evidently immaterial—until after signing on the dotted line!

the benefits of this survival has been the opportunity to provide the subject-matter of this book.

It would be nice to be able to report a similar long and successful life for his two folboat partners during Tug's Mediterranean adventures, Bombardier Brittlebank and Marine Hughes. But Fate has willed it otherwise in the case of Brittlebank. Tug last saw him at the Buckingham Palace investiture in 1946, receiving the Distinguished Conduct Medal which he so richly deserved. Not very long after that came the cruel and tragic news that, after all that he had accomplished and endured during the war, he had met his death in an accident while peacefully cycling in his native Nottinghamshire.

Marine Hughes, who accompanied Tug on the majority of his folboat expeditions from submarines in 1941, re-established contact with Tug Wilson in 1950, following a BBC programme in which they both featured, but a letter to him from Tug in 1982 was returned to sender. Perhaps the emergence of this book will cause him to surface once more? Although he is called Marine Hughes throughout this book, the strong probability is that he reached higher rank after Tug and he were split up in 1942. Tug remembers strenuous efforts at that time to arrange for his overdue promotion, but as he was a Marine everything had to be done through the correct Marine channels via Plymouth, and this required time.

\*

Guy Greville MC, whose surfacing, following the publication of *Night Train to Innsbruck*, led to the emergence of Tug Wilson's story, not only survived the war but is, forty-two years after his successful escape, serving on the East Cornwall District Council. On reaching Switzerland in 1943, after reporting to the ex-prisoner-of-war reception centre at Wil, he was put in charge of a camp for *évadés*, with two other officers (one British and one Australian), a New Zealand sergeant-major, six NCOs and a hundred and forty other ranks. All went smoothly, apart from some recalcitrant Aussies who decided to ignore the curfew regulations and had to be accommodated for a while in an emergency 'cooler'.

Soon after the Allied landings in the south of France, in August 1944, Guy was chosen with three other officers to find their way into France, via Geneva and Annécy, in order to link up with the French

Resistance and later with the American General Patch, whose army was moving up from the Mediterranean coast towards the Belfort Gap, between the Jura and the Vosges mountains. Guy eventually reached St Tropez, whence he embarked on a strangely indirect journey home. He was flown in a United States fighter-bomber to Ajaccio, in Corsica, and thence on to Naples, where he boarded a troopship carrying two hundred other ex-prisoners-of-war, bound via Algiers for Liverpool. But at least he was home for Christmas.

Like many returning former prisoners-of-war from Switzerland, Guy Greville was now eager for some more action. He promptly volunteered for service in the Far East and travelled by boat to India. VJ Day found him in a tank-landing-craft for an assault on the west coast of Malaya. The timely dropping of the two atom bombs, on Hiroshima and Nagasaki, rendered the assault unnecessary and the landing unopposed. But Guy's soldiering days were not quite over. He remained on the Reserve list and immediately volunteered for the abortive Suez affair in 1956. He only got as far as Cyprus.

The story of Peter McDowall, the young Ceylon tea-planter who matched Guy Greville's brave and acrobatic feat on the prisoner-of-war cattle-truck, ended alas in Switzerland. Soon after his arrival there he was smitten with polio and died in the friendly country that he had striven so hard and successfully to reach.

*

Captain Desmond Haslehust, MID (three times), who like Guy Greville escaped from Tug Wilson's train at Modena, and later ended up in Tug's last two camps in Germany, soldiered on with the Worcestershire Regiment after the war and reached the rank of major. He then answered the call to become a priest – his sojourn with Don Domenico Veronesi at Fosse, in the hills above Verona, having made a lasting impression on him. It was only fitting that, after a year's training at Downside Abbey followed by four years of further training in Rome, he should return to Fosse to celebrate his first Mass in the village where he was, and still is, so well known. His friend and mentor, Don Domenico Veronesi died at the age of ninety-eight in 1983, less than two years after Desmond Haslehust's last visit to him. A relief plaque can now be seen on the outside wall of Fosse church, to the left of the entrance door, in his memory.

Another of Desmond Haslehust's wartime helpers, in the mountain hotel above Fosse, Luciano Dal Cero the partisan leader, achieved lasting fame, to the extent of having a street in Verona named after him. He was a hero of the last battle for Verona between the Partisans and the retreating Germans, in the spring of 1945. He was awarded a posthumous Medaglio d'Oro, the Italian equivalent to the Victoria Cross.

Desmond's years as a parish priest have been spent in the south-west of England – in Dorchester, his home town Plymouth, Liskeard, Exmouth and now Axminster, with summer duty in the Scilly Isles. In 1981, by now The Very Reverend Canon Haslehust, he returned to Rome for a visit to mark his Silver Jubilee as a priest, and shook hands with Pope John Paul, little knowing that the latter was to come so near to death only a week later, from a fanatic's bullet.

*

Pip Gardner, VC, MC, Tug Wilson's fellow-fugitive in Rome in 1943, and fellow-prisoner in Regina Coeli, Luckenwalde, Märisch-Trubau and Brunswick, returned safely home eventually to civilian life after the war. While prospering and becoming Chairman and Managing Director, on his father's death in 1955, of his family's firm of air-conditioning equipment manufacturers, Pip also remained true to his wartime vow to help establish a Boy's Club in London, serving first as a Trustee from 1946 of the newly founded Brunswick Boys' Club in Fulham, and later occupying the position of Honorary Chairman for fourteen years, before becoming President in 1985 – information which he, typically, did not disclose, but which only emerged after further probing.

In addition to his active involvement with the Brunswick Boys' Club, Pip has been a member for many years of the Victoria Cross and George Cross Association of which he is now Honorary Secretary – the Chairman being Rear-Admiral Godfrey Place, VC, CB, DSC, who as a wartime submariner was known to Tug Wilson in their days with 10 Submarine Flotilla on Malta. In fact, he it was who helped Tug out of his folboat during his fateful transfer from *Upholder* to *Unbeaten* in 1942.

Pip Gardner has kept in touch with Tug Wilson ever since their return from their respective wartime escapades – modest heroes and great survivors both.

*

Major Sam Derry, as he appears in this book (later Colonel S. I. Derry, DSO, MC, JP, DL) duly returned to his native Newark in Nottinghamshire after the war. Forty years after the Liberation of Rome, he and twelve other members of the Rome Organisation attended a Reunion among their old haunts from May 30th to June 6th 1984 – converging from the USA, Canada, South Africa, Britain and Italy. Included in a sequence of gatherings and receptions in Rome was a visit to Regina Coeli prison, once only too familiar to all of them, whether from bitter inside experience, or from the menacing form of its forbidding exterior.

Of those mentioned in this story, Lieutenant John Furman (later Lieutenant-Colonel J. Furman, OBE, MC) and Lieutenant Bill Simpson (later Major W. C. Simpson, MC) were also present at this first Reunion of the Organisation that they had served so well. They and Sam Derry were interviewed in situ several times by an American Broadcasting Corporation TV camera crew throughout their stay.

At an Audience with the Pope all of them shook hands with His Holiness, who spoke to Sam Derry about the Rome Organisation and mentioned it in his speech in English. Uppermost in their minds, no doubt, was the memory of Monsignor Hugh O'Flaherty, OBE, who had helped them all in the dark days of 1943, before later handing over control of the Organisation to Sam Derry. After the war he became the senior official in the Vatican's Holy Office until 1960, when ill-health forced him to retire. Three years later, at the age of sixty-five, he died in Eire at the home of his widowed sister, Mrs Sheeham, at Cahirciveen in County Kerry, where he was buried – but not forgotten by the many whom he had helped.

*

The third and final instalment of the saga of Tug Wilson's silver compact is both happy and reassuring. A few weeks after he had bought the compact as a Christmas present for his wife in December 1943, he was arrested and relieved of his purchase when he was searched in Regina Coeli gaol. He ruefully thought that he had seen the last of it. To his great surprise, and to the considerable credit of his succession of gaolers, in April 1945, when Brunswick Camp was liberated by the advancing troops, the missing compact was returned to him to take home in triumph to his wife, Marjorie. When one considers Tug's movement from camp to camp in those chaotic times, the restoration of the solid silver compact to its rightful owner surely says a lot for the basic honesty of Tug's German captors – thereby providing hope for the future.

It is also pleasing, in view of Tug's long-standing and unwavering high regard for his wartime comrades, to be able to record that after the war he was made an Honorary Submariner, thus being able to attend reunions and meet fellow-survivors, tragically all too few in number, of the submarines that conveyed him to his stirring deeds in the Mediterranean in 1941 and 1942. To this day he remembers with great admiration and affection those brave captains and crews who took him to their hearts, among whom he was always made to feel an equal and so very much at home.

After going on wartime patrol in no less than nine different submarines out of Malta and Alexandria, several of which subsequently failed to return to base, Tug Wilson was indeed lucky to survive. Fortunate, too, is the fact that he lived to tell his tale and share his experiences with others.

# Index

# Index

185

Burma, 76

*Cachalot*, HMS/M, 36
Cahirciveen, 180
Cairo, 30, 36, 56, 58, 60, 71
Calabria, 62, 67, 91
Calato, 61
Calitri, 75
Camberley, 23
Cameron, Lt. J. L. 136–147
Campbell, Brigadier Jock, 132
Campbell, Sir Malcolm, 55
Cape Town, 28
Capua POW Camp, 85
Carabinieri, 67, 70, 76, 79, 119
Carlo Magno Pass, 120
Carthage, 51, 52
Casana Pass, 125–127
Cassibile, 84
Catania, 16
Catanzaro, 70, 71
Cayley, Lt-Cdr Dick, 43, 59
Ceylon, 13, 178
Ceylon Planters Rifles, 108
Chad, 56
Chamberlain, Neville, 21
Chieti POW Camp, 85, 132, 154, 156, 159
Churchill, Capt Randolph, 28
Churchill, Winston, 14, 16, 23, 24, 42, 47, 60
Clifton, 21, 23
Clogstoun-Willmott, Lt-Cdr, 30
Coed-y-Brenin, 23
Colditz POW Camp, 74
Collegio Teutonicum, 153, 155, 161
Cologne, 173
Colonne, Cape, 67
Combined Operations, 55, 56
Combined Operations (ME) 30, 31, 56
Commando Association, 14
**Commandos:**
No. 2, 75
No. 3, 26, 84

No. 4, 84
No. 7, 27
No. 8, 24, 27, 29
No. 11, 27, 29
Como, Lake, 120
*Conte Rosse*, 51
Corno d'Aquiglio, 142
Corrie, 27
Corsica, 178
Country Landowners' Association, 176
Courtney, G. B. 63
Courtney, Capt. R. J. A., 25, 26, 28, 30, 32, 41, 48, 54, 174
Coventry, 176
Crete, 29
Crotone, 62, 63, 67, 69, 70, 71
Cunningham, Admiral, 48
Cyprus, 178
Cyrenaica, 28
Czechoslovakia, 21, 169

Dal Cero, Luciano, 140, 179
Danube, River, 24
Dar-es-Salaam, 29
Deane-Drummond, Lt. A., 75, 76
De Burgh, Lt-Col, 159
Derna, 84
Derry, Major S. 154–156, 159, 160, 166, 180
Devonshire Regiment, 54
Dieppe, 26, 84, 171
Dimaro, 120
Dolgelley/Dolgellau, 23
Dorchester, 179
Dorset, 55
Dover, 23
Downside Abbey, 178
Dresden, 167, 169
Duke of Wellington's Regt., 84
Dunkirk, 22, 23
Durban, 28
Durnford-Slater, Lt-Col. J., 26, 84

East Cornwall District Council, 178